The LightHearted Soldier

CANADIAN'S EXPLOITS WITH THE BLACK DEVILS IN WW II

Herb Peppard

NIMBUS
PUBLISHING LTD

Nimbus Publishing Limited
PO Box 9301, Station A
Halifax, NS B3K 5N5
(902) 455-4286

Design: Arthur B. Carter
Cover design & illustration: Ivan Murphy
Printed and bound in Canada

Canadian Cataloguing in Publication Data

Peppard, Herb, 1920-
The lighthearted soldier
ISBN 1-55109-067-8
1. Peppard, Herb, 1920- 2. First Special Service Force—Biography.
3. Parachute troops—Biography. 4. World War, 1939-1945—
Personal narratives, Canadian. I. Title.
D811.P47 1994   940.54'1271'092   C94-950118-2

To my wife, Greta.
To me, she was the bravest, the sweetest,
the most beautiful woman who ever lived.
And to our children, Herbie, Lark, and Rosalee.

Acknowledgements

Many thanks to the following friends
who donated pictures:
Jim Anderson, Garfield Brown, Peter Gottingham, Sid
County, Linda Fornier, Jim Gilbert, Ben Gray, John
Landriault, Bob Macon, Hector MacInnis, Tom Perry,
George Tratt, Alan "Spud" Wright, George Wright.
And to Lieutenant Colonel Robert D. Burhans,
author of *First Special Service Force*.

Contents

First group of Canadians to go to Fort Benning, Georgia, for parachute training. Herb Peppard is third from right, second row. Photograph taken at Lansdown Park, Ottawa, July 1942. (National Archives of Canada)

Introduction

The First Special Service Force in which author Herb Peppard and I both served, was unique. It was the sole parachute-ski-command-type unit of the World War II Allied Armies. Its combat echelon consisted of both American and Canadian Army volunteers. (There was also a U.S. Service Battalion which took care of most housekeeping needs because the combat echelon spent all its time training under an accelerated program.)

The original idea OK'd by Prime Minister Winston Churchill of Great Britain and President Franklin D. Roosevelt of the United States was a unit equipped with a special vehicle to fight in snowy terrain in Norway, Italy, and Rumania—all critical to the Axis war effort. The concept was beyond Britain's capacity to organize and equip. The United States agreed to do it. The Canadians were invited to participate.

In the summer of 1942, a call went out to U.S. and Canadian Army units for paratroop volunteers. In Canada, most who responded—like Herb Peppard—joined the 1st Canadian Parachute Battalion. They took their parachute training in the United States, because Canada didn't have the facilities at that time. Later, Peppard, along with many of the others, transferred to the shadowy 2nd Canadian Parachute Battalion. These Canadian volunteers soon found themselves totally integrated with U.S. Army volunteers into a secret unit called the First Special Service Force.

That's where Herb Peppard's initial airborne experiences differ from mine. While he was with the 1st Canadian Parachute Battalion jumping at Ft. Benning, Ga., I went directly to the First Special Service Force at Ft. William Henry Harrison, Helena, Montana, where Canadians were already being trained side-by-side with American soldiers. On arrival at Ft. Harrison, volunteers were assigned to Force regiments and companies, and found themselves sharing a tent with two American volunteers.

In late 1942, the difficulties of the Canadian Army in providing replacements for those injured and otherwise shipped out forced an appeal for volunteers from the 1st Canadian Parachute Battalion in Ft. Benning. Herb Peppard was one of that group.

On arrival at Ft. Harrison, he was assigned to 1st Company, First Regiment. (I was in 4th Company, Second Regiment.) He was measured for an American uniform and issued the distinguishing Force insignia—a bright red shoulder patch that read USA-Canada in white letters and lapel discs—one set with embossed Crossed Arrows, the other with Canada stamped on them. (Americans of the Force had U.S. discs.) A red, white, and blue shoulder cord made of parachute shroud lines, a cap with red, white, and blue piping, and a red, white, and blue oval to go behind our U.S. style parachute wings, made up our dress uniform—that plus our tall, brown, Corcoran jump boots, into which we bloused the bottoms of our trousers.

We trained to use American weapons because the Force would be totally supplied by the U.S. Army. We were taught to be expert demolitionists, using a new high explosive called RS. We underwent a special type of hand-to-hand combat taught by a former Inspector of the Shanghai Police named "Pat" O'Neil.

The mountainous terrain of Montana was ideal for teaching mountaineering. We spent weeks of climbing rock faces and rappelling down them.

With winter closing in, out came the skis, as well as our

tracked snow vehicle—the Weasel. Ski trainers were Norwegians who had escaped after Hitler's invasion of their country. We promptly dubbed them Ski-wegians, after spending hours, days, and weeks learning how to use our "torture-boards" carrying full loads of ammunition, weapons, food, sleeping gear, and the like.

For various reasons, by January, 1943, the original missions of the Force had been canceled. April saw the Force board trains and head for Norfolk, Virginia, where we learned amphibious landing techniques using landing craft and rubber boats. It was a heady Spring experience after a tough Montana winter. This was quickly followed by a shift to Fort Ethan Allen, Burlington, Vt., for small unit tactics and inspection by the Inspectors General of both armies. Force scores went to the top of the charts. The Force was ready for combat.

In late June, Forcemen entrained West again to San Franciso Harbor, and from thence to the Aleutian Islands. The Japanese were about to be kicked off their remaining Aleutian conquest—Kiska. Forcemen spearheaded the attack on the night of August 15, 1943, hours in advance of the main bodies, and found the Japanese had fled. Only two days later, the Force was aboard transports, heading back to the U.S., thence to the Mediterranean Theater.

By December 3, Forcemen in Italy were climbing a mountain mass that had stalled the U.S. Fifth Army for weeks. Aptly named Monte La Difensa, it was the key to the German Winter Lines, and was well defended. Force leadership decided that the best way to assault this stronghold was up escarpment—some 150 feet—that would place Second Regiment in back of the German defenses, and hopefully create total surprise. Laden with all their weapons, food, ammunition, and ropes, Second Regiment made the ascent in pitch black night, roping its way up the walls to the bowl-shaped area on top.

At dawn, 1st Battalion, Second Regiment, attacked. Feet

slipping on loose shale alerted the Germans, and a vicious fire fight was on. Within a little over two hours, the peak had been captured—Army planners had figured it would take at least two days. The Force held in the face of strong counter-attacks. It then went on to capture adjacent Monte La Remetanea.

On Christmas Day, 1943, we crossed the valley, and First Regiment, despite its losses on Difensa, helped take another guardian mountain. Then while American, British, and Italian infantry units battled up the valley and the foothills, Forcemen fought across trackless mountain wastes in battle after battle in the worst Italian winter in memory. Radicosa, Monte Majo, and Mount Vischiataro overlooking Monte Cassino, were the major Force battles recorded, with hundreds of smaller skirmished and attacks making up the whole.

Tired and depleted, Forcemen no sooner had settled into their base camp to recoup and refit, when word came they were needed on the Anzio Beachhead. Darby's Rangers had been virtually wiped out and the Force had to plug the gap. Much under strength, (1200 men—a ratio of only one man per twelve yards of coverage), the Force took over one-quarter of the entire Beachhead perimeter—a division-sized chunk. Forcemen were on the front line for over three months without relief. All regiments carried out aggressive patrolling. Only in this way, could the Germans be kept in ignorance of our true strength on the ground, and be prevented from sweeping through us as they were trying to do at the end of the Beachhead.

Finally pulled off the line in May, the Force rested, received replacements to bring it up to strength, and studied plans for the next phase—a break-out from the Beachhead and the capture of Rome. On May 25, First Regiment hit the German lines, breaking through and moving so fast the U.S. 3rd Division on the left flank was unable to keep up, which opened a dangerous gap on First's flank. Down the gap rode German tanks, and it was only with heavy losses that the Regiment was able to pull back. The advance was resumed the next day.

On June 4, 1944, soldiers of the First Special Service Force were the first Allied troops to penetrate Rome in strength, driving the German rearguard before them as they captured seven bridges over the River Tiber and led Allied Armies into the first major Axis city to fall.

The Force joined the 7th U.S. Army as it prepared for a major amphibious invasion of Southern France. On August 15, 1944, a year to the day from the Force's dry-run landing on Kiska, First Regiment rubber-boated ashore to capture Port Cros, one of two island in the Hyeres group. Second and Third Regiments landed on a second and larger island—Levant. Arriving at both islands in the early morning, four or five hours before the mainland attack, as on Kiska, the Force captured and neutralized each in time for the rest of the 7th Army to land, safe from a rear attack.

Once on the mainland, the three regiments marched and battled their way to the Franco-Italian border—the line between the Mediterranean and the European Theaters of War.

Relieved November 20, 1944, the Force was stationed at Villeneuve-Loubet, near Nice, where Forcemen were stunned to learn the unit was being disbanded. The time for small special units was past. Armies and army groups were wheeling and fighting in Northern Europe. The Canadian Army was in a manpower crisis.

On December 5, 1944, Canadians of the Force stepped out of ranks to form into the First Canadian Special Service Battalion. They marched off the field with a salute. Their American buddies stood at attention, leaving unfilled the gaps in their ranks caused by the departure of their friends.

In all its combat time, the Force never failed to attain its objectives. But, as one American said years later, when the

Canadians stepped out, the spirit of the Force was gone. It left a formidable legacy, now borne proudly in Canada by the Canadian Airborne Regiment, and in the United States by the U.S. Army Special Forces (Green Berets).

Sholto Watt of the *Montreal Standard* later wrote: "I can testify to their spectacular power and efficiency, their marvelous morale, and their never-failing spirit of attack. . . . Their legend [is] a feat of arms which will remain celebrated in military history...."

And so it has.

William S. Story, CAE
Executive Director, FSSF Association
Moneta, Virginia

Chapter 1
The Reluctant Recruit

"The Germans are marching through Ziggo Solakia! The Germans are marching through Ziggo Solakia!" Bill MacKenzie shouted over and over as he ran across the railway tracks towards us. Bill's brother, "Bub," and I were piling lumber when we heard this startling news. It was March 1939. The three of us were working for the lumber company Spencer Brothers and Turner. Our work was repetitive and monotonous, but we were thankful to have any job in those hard times. The pay was meagre by today's standards. When I started there in 1936, my wage was fifteen cents an hour; three years later I was up to twenty-three cents. Working from 7:00 A.M. until 6:00 P.M., I made $2.30 per day—pretty good money at that time, for an eighteen-year-old.

Some days we'd pile green lumber to dry; other days, we'd load dry lumber onto wagons to go to the mill for planeing and finishing. Sometimes we'd load lumber into boxcars. No wonder we were excited when Bill brought us this world-shattering news. Something was happening outside the confines of this lumberyard and my hometown of Truro, Nova Scotia! We grabbed the *Halifax Herald* from Bill. It was true! Hitler had started his conquest of Europe. He had annexed the neighbouring country of Czechoslovakia.

As I read the paper, Bill kept shouting the headline, as best he could: "The Germans are marching through Ziggo Solakia! The Germans are marching through Ziggo Solakia!" I smiled to myself at his pronunciation of the foreign country. I felt somewhat superior, having an advanced education of grade

1

Doug King, Freeman Wallace (both served overseas with the North Nova Scotia Highlanders) and Herb at 18 years in Truro.

nine, compared to his grade four, but the truth was that I didn't know much more than he did. I knew that the country's name was Czechoslovakia and that it was somewhere in Europe. Beyond that it was all a blank.

To me, this world-shaking news was not only exciting—it

was scary! I had seen newsreels and movies about the world war, and there seemed to be nothing romantic or chivalrous about it. I'd also read *All Quiet on the Western Front*—the story of a soldier who had outlived most of his buddies through the war, only to be killed weeks before it ended when he reached out from his trench to pick a beautiful flower that had miraculously survived amidst the desolation. Later that day an army communiqué cryptically reported on the occurrences of the day: "All quiet on the Western Front."

The symbolic irony of this popular anti-war novel made a big impression on me. War seemed useless and futile, and in war an individual life—including mine—was unimportant. I made a silent vow not to go to war unless I absolutely had to. Instead, I endured the monotony of the lumberyard. Even after Hitler's army invaded Poland, and Canada declared war, I stubbornly piled lumber.

While I worked away, Truro became ever livelier. Men in army uniform became a common sight. Barrett, a former teacher, donned a smart officer's uniform. The militia members were instantly called up. Many were taken right from their jobs at such places as Stanfield's and the Eastern Hat and Cap Factory. Amidst all the bustle, it soon became obvious that Canada was pathetically ill-equipped for a world conflict. As hundreds of men and boys from Truro flocked to the recruiting station, the shortages became increasingly apparent. There were soldiers without army boots, and even soldiers without weapons! Such a sight did little for civilian morale.

Then came the scare about the "fifth columnists"—traitorous saboteurs rumoured to be in our midst. The army took this security threat very seriously and determined that the most important place to guard was the train bridge over the Salmon River. Over that strategic span had to pass all the trains travelling from Upper Canada to Halifax—trains that would carry soldiers, food, and war supplies to Halifax and thence to Britain.

The appointed guards were boys I knew, only recently turned soldiers, so after work, Freeman Wallace and I went over to the bridge for a look. Four soldiers marched back and forth across the bridge. One wore an oversized uniform from the Great War and carried a rifle from the same era. The other three had no uniforms at all. They wore peaked caps and civilian clothes. In place of rifles, they carried short poles. One carried a broom, at his shoulder, in the way soldiers do when marching.

Freeman and I knew this fledgling soldier well. He looked so ridiculous that we started poking fun at him, but he never let on that he saw us. He maintained his determined military stride, marching back and forth across the bridge. His eyes were fixed straight ahead; his back was stiff as a ramrod. Freeman and I had no sympathy for these seemingly play-soldiers. We didn't realize until we joined the army ourselves, that a soldier does what he's told, no matter how ridiculous the order. To us it looked like a comical farce, so we shouted many nasty things. Our most brilliant gibe was: "Hey, Harold! If the Germans come, what ya gonna do, sweep them off the bridge?"

As we were walking home talking about the bridge, a vivid picture flashed through my mind. In grade eight we had studied a poem about brave Horatius saving ancient Rome. A huge army was descending on the city. Rome seemed doomed. The town fathers felt that the only salvation was to hew down the bridge that invaders must use to cross the Tiber River. But the enemy would be upon them, it seemed, before the bridge could be destroyed. Horatius then stepped forward and said that because the bridge was straight and narrow, it could be defended by three men. Two others stepped forward, and the three patriots defended the bridge against the might of the invading army. They fought and fought, even

Brand new soldier! Herb Peppard and his youngest brother Bill, in 1941, soon after Herb signed up.

after being wounded. They held out until the bridge came down and Rome was saved.

My thoughts returned to the Salmon River train bridge and the four stalwarts guarding it. I suddenly imagined one hundred or more saboteurs attacking the train bridge. They were all dressed in beige trench coats, with dark hats pulled low on their foreheads. Their canes became sharp, brutal-looking swords. They yelled obscenities in German as they rushed the gallant defenders. In my mind's eye, Harold had rushed to the forefront to take the brunt of the attack. With his broomstick thrust out before him, he strove to drive the enemy back, but the flashing swords kept whittling away his broom until he held only the bristles tucked under his arm. Then my dream faded, just in time to save Harold and the bridge. I was jolted back to reality when Freeman said, "What if we got in the army and we got Harold as our sergeant? My God! He'd give us a hard time, wouldn't he?" It was a sobering thought, but I dismissed this disturbing vision by saying: "We'll cross that bridge when we come to it." Then we laughed like fools all the rest of the way home.

Soon after came the most shocking news we had ever heard: France had fallen! We had been led to believe that the huge French army and the impregnable Maginot Line could withstand any onslaught. Now, we learned that France had been crushed in a few weeks by the awesome German blitzkrieg! Even after this stunning news, I kept on working at the lumberyard.

Then came the Battle of Britain. We had heard on the radio and seen on the newsreels how powerful the German air force was. It was said that Goering had vowed to Hitler that his mighty Luftwaffe would knock England out of the war in a matter of weeks. As wave after wave of German planes descended on England the future looked bleak indeed. I stuck stubbornly to my vow not to fight, but my resolve was slowly weakening. I began thinking that I was missing out on something big—something history-making, world-shattering! I began to feel conspicuous by my presence. I was young, healthy, and able-bodied, and there weren't many such people left in Truro.

What finally shamed me into joining up was the troop trains—those damned troop trains! The lumberyard was close to the railway tracks and the station. Many of the troop trains would slow down, or stop, opposite where we were working, while awaiting their turn to go into the station. There were hundreds of trains, carrying tens of thousands of servicemen to Halifax, from where they would sail for England. The passenger cars were covered with signs: "Hitler, here we come"; "Next stop, Berlin!" and many more. One miserable day, in December 1940, a troop train stopped just across from where I was loading a wagon. Bub Mackenzie was sliding lumber down to me from a high pile. It had snowed the night before, and now the snow was melting. As I took the planks from Bub, ice-cold water ran down the lumber, up my arms, onto my jacket, and into my face. Just then I heard the jeers from the soldiers hanging out the train windows: "Sucker!" Looking at them, all warm and cosy and dry in their heavy uniforms, I felt a twinge of envy. My resolve evaporated into the morning air. My mind was made up. Canadian Army, here I come! Freeman and I joined up the next day.

Chapter 2

Rest Easy Canada, I've Joined the Army!

"The army will make a man of you," my dad had said, but after being in it for two weeks, and antagonizing most of my superiors, I wondered if he'd been wrong.

The day I volunteered, I was rudely introduced to army life. I stood shivering in a long line-up waiting for my medical examination. It was December, and the cavernous old armoury was unheated, but the main reason we shivered was we were all naked. A fearsome looking sergeant had ordered us to remove our clothes. I tried to talk casually with the naked stranger next to me, but I was excruciatingly embarrassed. I would have given anything for a blanket, or even a towel. I tried to act nonchalant. I leaned against a wall, still chatting, but uncertain where to put my hands. Throwing caution to the winds, I clasped them behind my back, but I felt so immediately vulnerable that I quickly clasped them in front of me. Probably they do this with all recruits as indoctrination, I thought to myself, but the thought gave me little comfort.

The medical officer further embarrassed me by prodding and poking some of the most delicate parts of my body. When, finally, he nodded, and said gruffly that I had passed my physical, I rushed to retrieve my precious clothes.

x x x

As a new recruit I didn't know the limits of a sergeant's authority, but whenever one of them screamed at me it frightened me, and, knowing no better, I was willing to take orders from anyone wearing a uniform. Nor did I understand

(and I still don't) why they sounded so angry. I certainly did nothing—at least during my first days in the army—to antagonize a sergeant! On the contrary, I stood quietly, attentively, nervously—ready to obey any order flung at me.

The apparently angry yelling gave me a flashback to my school days and I recalled my first male teacher. I was in grade seven, and I had to take weekly classes in manual training— the study of woodworking and mechanical drawing. The teacher was a big, gruff man, by the name of David L. Whitby. He spoke crossly to me only once, but that was enough. Win MacIntosh, one of my classmates, wanted to use the circular saw but didn't know how to set it up properly, or how to start it. I went over to help him, but I knew only slightly more than he did. We were fiddling around with the machine when we heard a bellow from right behind us that must have been heard from as far as the Truro Amateur Athletic Club nearly a mile away. "Boy! Boy!" yelled Mr. Whitby, "If you don't know anything about the machinery, *leave it alone!*" We were in manual training for three years, and I don't think Win or I ever touched that saw again.

The sergeants whom I encountered during my first weeks in the army were fearful figures to me, particularly Sergeant MacDougal whose official authority was heightened by an innate gift for intimidation. To him I owe my introduction to the military principle of instilling obedience through fear.

x x x

Late that afternoon, we boarded the train at the Truro station, bound for Halifax. We arrived after dark, and we were loaded into two army trucks and driven to our new "home"— a long barracks, heated by two pot-bellied stoves. One stove was glowing cherry-red, and the other was billowing black smoke from the unignited coal. On either side of the centre aisle was a row of double-tier bunks. "Toss your belongings on one of the bunks, and then get over to the mess hall for chow!" yelled our newly acquired corporal. I welcomed this order, but my first look at army grub made me question further my decision to join the army. The main course was two pieces of toast smothered with hot, canned tomatoes, with two slabs of bacon on top. This "meal," I soon learned was known as "red lead and bacon" or, less affectionately, "shit on a shingle." The only drink was tea—in a big Dixie cup. This was difficult for me, because I was used to milk at mealtimes. Dessert was a mushy goo that we were told was bread pudding, but which looked so unappetizing that I had to smell it, cautiously, before I'd go near it.

We returned to barracks still hungry. I flopped down and fell right to sleep. I was awakened, abruptly, by the loudest, harshest noise I had ever heard. I sat bolt upright, smashing my head against the bunk above me. Then I saw the source of the disturbance—a perfect looking soldier, with a bugle pressed to his lips, standing at the foot of my bed. A glint of demonic joy shone in his eyes as he puffed his cheeks out like a giant bullfrog and shattered the tranquillity of sleep. The bugler was followed, immediately, by a huge man with three stripes on each sleeve. "I'm Sergeant MacDougal!" he yelled, as though we were all deaf. Everyone jumped to attention awaiting his next holler. "Form up outside, to march over for medical inspection." We tumbled over each other in haste to obey this great, ugly person, who seemed to have more power than King George himself.

At the medical office we were ordered to undress again. The medical officer (MO) looked me all over very closely. "Have you been sick?" he asked. "No," I answered. When he pointed to two pips on his shoulder, I quickly blurted out, "No, sir!" "Well, I'm sorry soldier, but you have German measles. You'll have to go to hospital and be quarantined." *German measles,* what irony, I thought. I had joined the Canadian Army to save the world and the enemy had struck me down in less than twenty-four hours. Maybe this dreaded disease was one of their secret weapons. "German measles!"

I muttered in disbelief as I was rushed to the army hospital on Cogswell Street, where I was dropped unceremoniously at the door to fend for myself.

Still in civilian clothes, I stood at the admitting desk. A nurse, scarcely looking up over her horn-rimmed glasses, started to fill out a form. "Name?" she asked in such a crisp military manner that I felt I should be standing at attention. "Herbert Peppard," I answered. "Number?" Number? What number, I wondered? I gave her my home address. "Seventeen Alice Street, Truro." "No! No! Your regimental number," she said impatiently. I didn't remember having been given one. "I don't know my number," I said slowly with an embarrassed smile. With this, she finally did look me full in the face, and I wondered again why all these army superiors looked so unfriendly. "Where are you stationed?" she asked. "In a barracks," I came back lamely. "I imagine so," she snorted sarcastically. "But where is the barracks? What's the name of your camp?" Again I had to answer that I didn't know. I'd only been there to eat and sleep. I'd had no time to get information. "I don't know the name of the camp or where it is," I answered apologetically. She was getting very exasperated, so I prayed that I'd be able to answer her next question, but this was not to be. "What's the name of your unit?" she fired at me. My God! Why didn't she ask something easy, like—"Who was the third premier of Nova Scotia?" At least I could have guessed at that. "I don't know," I whispered.

That was the last straw. Slamming her pencil down she yelled for the ward-boy. "Take this patient to Ward Three, and make sure he doesn't get lost." "Miss Nightingale" heaved a great sigh of relief as I hurried down the hall, and before I could completely escape she said, loudly, to someone: "I'm surprised he remembered his *name*! He didn't know his regimental number, where he was stationed, or the name of his unit. All I can say is, thank God we still have our navy!"

I stayed in hospital for eight days without learning my

regimental number, my unit, or where I was stationed, but on the eighth day a truck miraculously arrived to take me back to camp. How they knew when to come I haven't a clue.

I made it my business to find out, as quickly as I could, that I was stationed at Connolly Street Barracks; my unit was the Fourteenth Anti-Aircraft Battery, and my regimental number was F85014. The next day, I was issued a uniform, helmet, and rifle. Everything was about four sizes too big, even my steel helmet, which continually slipped down over my eyes. Our unit was helping to defend the provincial capital, and I often thought, then and later, that had I been called upon at that stage of my army career, poor old Halifax would have been in deep, deep trouble.

My tribulations started in earnest the next day when I was approached by Corporal Innis. "You're on guard at the front gate today," he grunted. I started to protest, but he stopped me short. "You'll never learn younger." This seemed quite philosophical for a man with such a rough exterior. "But I've never even had rifle drill." I pleaded. The corporal shrugged off my protests and told me to get the hell out to my post.

It was—of course—a miserable day: the cold rain turned into big wet snowflakes every so often. The unpaved road outside the gate was a quagmire of potholes filled with muddy red water. I stood stiffly at attention for awhile, then marched the eight feet or so from one side of the gate to the other, trying to keep warm. I kept hoping that no one would approach, because I wasn't sure how to challenge an intruder.

My worst fears were soon realized. The quiet morning was shattered by the roar of a motorcycle. I saw rider, motorcycle, and sidecar bouncing up and down over the muddy potholes and spraying red-coloured water on either side as they approached the gate. He came close enough that I could see he was a lieutenant, before his wheel suddenly dropped into an oversized pothole—and stayed there. He got off and started to push and tug, but the motorcycle wouldn't budge.

Without hesitation, I rushed out to help the stranded officer and unwittingly violated the most basic military tenet: Never leave your post unguarded! Hitler and half the German army could have marched through that gate unchallenged! Lucky for me, they weren't aware of their opportunity.

In my eagerness to be a good Samaritan, I almost put down my rifle, but I stopped myself in the act. The ground was covered with mud and water, and a soldier's weapon was his most precious possession. He must strive to keep it in perfect working condition, which meant spotlessly clean. I thought, smugly, that I had begun to learn about soldiering.

I looked feverishly around and saw a schoolboy approaching carrying his books. I hailed him, shoved the rifle into his hands and said, "Hold this for a minute!" He was so excited that he almost dropped his books into the mud, and he cradled the rifle with great pride in the crook of his arms. No doubt he felt, like me, that he was contributing a great deal toward the successful culmination of the world conflict.

In no time, the lieutenant and I freed his motorcycle, and he went through the gate with a wave of his hand and a hearty "thanks." I recovered my rifle from the boy, who seemed reluctant to part with it, and kept asking, "Is it loaded?" I left him standing there with the question unanswered and rushed back towards my post. I didn't quite make it, however, because I came face to face with the very angry Sergeant MacDougal. His booming voice not only frightened but embarrassed me, because I was certain that my friends stationed a mile away at Citadel Hill could hear him. "What in the hell's the matter with you?" he thundered, his face so close to mine that our noses nearly touched, and I could see the sparks of anger in his eyes. "I've been in this man's army fifteen years, and I never saw anything so stupid in my entire life! Not only did you leave your post unguarded, but you handed your rifle, your most precious possession in life, to a little kid on the side of the road!! My God! What kind of people are we getting in our army today?"

Having gotten this off his chest, he exploded with the inevitable question. "How long have you been in the army soldier?" I came proudly to attention, and answered, as smartly as possible: "Two days, sergeant." That didn't impress him, and he shouted back immediately: "That's no excuse! And from now on I'll be keeping a close eye on you. Another infraction and you'll be up on the carpet before the Old Man, and that's a promise! You kids have been babied and catered to long enough. You're in the army now, and just a word of warning. You may have been able to break your mother's heart, but you'll *never break mine!*"

And I found out that he was right, just as all superiors are always right in the army.

Chapter 3
Woodard: One of a Kind!

My unit's major weapons for defending Halifax were two, three-inch, anti-aircraft guns, but as most of us were green recruits I often felt that should any German aircraft decide to land in the field across the road, our barrage probably wouldn't even graze their wingtips. So when Woodard, his very good friend George Beers, and five or six others, were transferred from a New Brunswick infantry unit—the Carleton and York Regiment—they seemed almost veterans to me. Why they were transferred they never said, and I never asked. And Woodard's considerable experience, we soon learned, was hardly of a military nature.

Woodard was a formidable looking man, big and very strong. He had a ruddy face, topped with a shock of black hair, and heavy black eyebrows that hung over a pair of active, dark eyes. His face reminded me somehow of Max Schmeling, the German heavyweight boxer who became a hero to the Nazis when he defeated the great Joe Louis but was forgotten after Louis knocked him out in their return match. Of course, I didn't tell Woodard of this resemblance! He was thirty-five years old and to me, being twenty, he seemed quite ancient. His friend, Beers, was close to thirty. He was also a big man—good-looking, with a shock of blond hair and sparkling blue eyes. He was as bright and jovial as Woodard was dark and temperamental. The two friends seemed like opposites, and they both fascinated me. Before long they took me into their confidence—I think it was because my character was somewhere between the two of them—and we became buddies until I left the unit.

I got my first taste of Woodard's headstrong individualism when I came back to barracks one winter evening. I'd been in downtown Halifax, at the Capital, watching the beautifully developed Jane Russell. The film—*The Outlaw*—was controversial; some thought it was too revealing and should be censored. I found it memorable—I can still see Miss Russell quite clearly, but the plot escapes me. I opened the barracks door and was nearly knocked over by dense smoke and the smell of burning leather. The source of the disorder was Woodard. He was standing at one of the pot-bellied stoves, running a red-hot poker back and forth over his black army boot, while a bunch of the men gathered around and watched approvingly. I was appalled, and terrified, by this apparent destruction of government property—and the possible consequences. Miss Russell was temporarily forgotten—here was a *real* outlaw, in our very midst. I looked anxiously over my shoulder expecting an officer to crash in with the military police and arrest us all. But no vengeful authority appeared, and Woodard calmly continued his odorous task.

Beers explained to me what his friend was doing. Our army boots had a pebbled surface and were saturated with some type of greasy preservative. This made it impossible to get a high-gloss shine on them. Singeing them with the hot poker removed the pebbles and grease. Then you could raise a shine on your boots that you could see your face in.

For the next three nights we had to endure a smelly, smoke-filled barracks. That's how long it took Woodard to treat every boot in the unit. Of course, he didn't do it out of the goodness of his heart. He was in business. He charged one dollar a pair—a sizeable sum when our wages were thirty dollars a month. But we had to pay up if we wanted to look as good as our buddies. Besides which, everyone thought it was a good idea, and we admired Woodard for doing something we hadn't thought of and wouldn't have had the nerve to do.

In 1941, our unit was moved to Isle Maligne, Quebec—about two hundred miles north of Quebec City—to protect a power plant. While there, Woodard came up with another entrepreneurial scheme—this one more doubtful. He became our barber! I don't think he had ever cut hair before, but he borrowed a big bowl from the cookhouse, bought a wire-bristled hairbrush and set up shop.

The strange thing was that we used his dubious services! He was very rough with his wire brush, pushing it into my scalp as though he were brushing down a horse. He'd run the brush into my scalp then adjust the bowl, all the while repeating his favourite ditty. It wasn't a song, it wasn't a poem, but he recited it as though it were a rhyme. It was a circus barker's sales pitch that Woodard had learned word for word. He repeated it so often that I memorized it myself. "Step right up, folks! Step this way! Come in and see the eighth wonder of the world! Come in and see Doh Doh, the Dog-faced Boy! No talks, no walks, but crawls on his belly like a human reptile! Come one, come all, only a dime, ten cents; neither make ya, break ya, or take ya to the Old Country and bring ya back ... Stand back, brother, ya bother me!"

Why did we put up with this? Partly because Woodard was the only "barber" around, but mainly because we couldn't resist his forceful personality. He charged twenty-five cents per haircut and could have built up some savings, but Woodard had a great weakness. He loved to drink and of course he did it to excess—which was his undoing. He'd go alone to town, on pass, and return late, very drunk, and disrupt the entire barracks. He'd tip over chairs, sing, curse, and shake a few people here and there, to make sure they knew Woodard was back. That was the bad side of his need to be the centre of attention.

On one occasion, I was sitting on the toilet leisurely reading a magazine at about one o'clock in the morning, when a terrific crash shook my little retreat. A big fist came smashing through the pressed cardboard wall and stopped right in front of my face. It was Woodard, of course. I helped extricate him from the wall, escorted him to his bunk, then returned to my seat—but my solitude was shattered.

After enduring several of these disturbances, Beers and I decided that it was time to teach Woodard a lesson. "Let's make a French bed for the silly old fool," Beers suggested. I thought that was a great idea, because Woodard always made his bed carefully before he went on pass, so that he could just crawl under the blankets when he got back and sleep it off. A French bed (I have never learned where the name comes from) is made by folding the bedclothes in half from bottom to top, then covering them with an extra blanket to conceal the trick. The victim can't get more than halfway into bed, because they're sitting on the bedclothes.

So we set our trap and lay awake, expectantly, until 1:15 in the morning when Woodard stumbled in. He fumbled out of his clothes, then, with a great sigh, heaved himself into his upper bunk. We couldn't see his face in the dark, but we could hear him begin to thresh around and make grunts of surprise and frustration. We could imagine him trying to figure it out and the look on his face; and that set us off laughing. Woodard started to curse, swear, and threaten, but he was too far gone to act. Finally, with a snort of disgust, he disengaged himself, pulled the top blanket over him, and was soon snoring loudly.

Beers and I laughed ourselves to sleep, but our prank had no further effect. We had feared a tongue-lashing, or worse but never a word from Woodard, who just carried on in his old ways. We realized that we'd been far too easy on this big, tough buddy of ours. We decided that we'd have to do something really vicious—something that would really embarrass him—if we expected to make him change his ways. We put our heads together and came up with the perfect scheme—something that even Woodard would never live down.

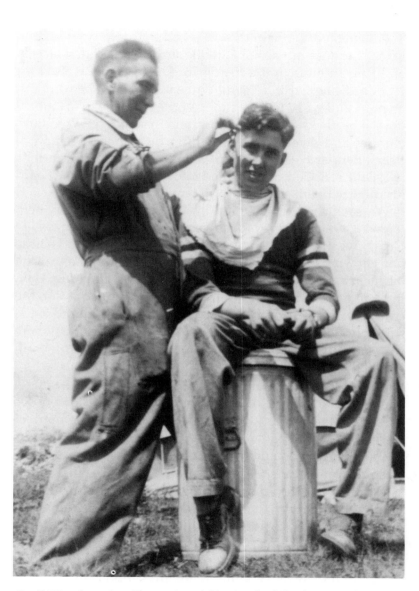

Cecil Woodward, self-appointed "barber" of the fourteenth Anti-Aircraft Battery, at work on private Jim Hennigar. "The strange thing was that we used his dubious services!"

We enlisted the help of two other big men, Harnish and Potter, because our scheme, while simple, depended largely on brute strength and a firm grip. Then we just waited for Woodard's next trip to town. Three nights later, he went out on pass, and we bided our time. A little after one in the morning the barracks door burst open and in staggered Woodard, cursing and swearing, and calling out: "Beers! Peppard! Beers! Peppard!" We just kept up our mock snoring until he fell silent, stripped, and crawled into bed. In no time we heard his mighty drunken snores and went into action.

We each took up position on a corner of the steel bed. (Newell, who occupied the lower bunk, was away on leave.) Gently we lifted the bed off the floor. Woodard stirred a little but kept on snoring. By this time, most of the men in the barracks were awake and trying to keep from laughing. Willing hands held the door open and we staggered out into the darkness. Ever so slowly, we traversed the two hundred yards from our barracks to the centre of the parade square, where we carefully set down poor, unfortunate Woodard—still sound asleep. Then we returned to bed.

We got little sleep, anticipating the first note of the bugle at sunrise. The crack of dawn found us all with our noses pressed to the window, gazing at the lonely looking bunk in the middle of the parade square. Woodard slept on. Finally, the bugler marched out. Lance-Corporal Johnson was a gung-ho soldier, and come hell or high water, the bugle must sound at sunrise. He glanced only momentarily at the bunk and its occupant, then, with a click of his heels, and straightening of his back, he came to attention. A quick bend of his elbow, a flick of the wrist, and the bugle was pressed firmly to his lips. With a maniacal grin he gave a shrill blast. It pierced the still morning air like a knife. Woodard sat bolt upright and looked in every direction. He saw the bugler; he saw the empty parade square; he wondered where he was and how he got there. Then, with a jerk, he stumbled down onto the

cement of the parade square in his shorts and undershirt. An instant later he pulled his blanket down, threw it around himself, and scuttled back to the barracks.

Our scheme worked beyond our expectations. From that day, Woodard was a changed man—at least in his drinking habits. The realization that he could be manhandled that way and not even know it really scared him. He would go to town, as before, but he never again came back to barracks so drunk that he didn't know what he was doing. I imagine that at the back of his mind ever lingered the vision of a cold dawn, an empty parade square, a noisy bugler, and himself shivering in an upper bunk.

I transferred out of the Fourteenth Anti-Aircraft Battery in the summer of 1942. I left Woodard and Beers and the rest of my buddies in Tor Bay, Newfoundland, and I've never seen Woodard or Beers again.

About thirty years after the war, my wife, Greta, and I were visiting my mother at Christmas. The phone rang and Mum answered it. "It's for you, Herbie." "This is Cecil Woodard calling," a familiar voice said. I immediately smelled the burning boots, felt the steel brush through my hair, remembered the painstaking workmanship of the French bed, and saw a steel bunk on an empty parade square on a cool fall morning. "Where are you, Woodard?" "I'm home," he said. "I'm still living in Woodstock, New Brunswick." "Well, what have you been doing?" "You wouldn't believe it, but I've been up north teaching Eskimos. I taught English and math, but not for long. One of my students was a fast learner, and when he learned how to count to one hundred, he took over my job. So they fired me, and I came home."

I didn't know what to make of that story, so I asked him what had happened to him during the war, after I'd left the unit. "Well, let me tell you ..." Woodard said, and launched into another strange story. He told me—at some length—how he and Beers had arrested an elderly man in Belgium because his overcoat bulged suspiciously. They marched him to the provost marshal, who was sceptical but ordered the man to unbutton his coat. He told me that what he and Beers had been certain was a machine gun turned out to be an umbrella. I couldn't decide, from his tone, whether these stories were true, or one of Woodard's jokes. I did find out that he had never gotten married, and that he hadn't been in touch with Beers for a long time, but little else about his life over the previous thirty years. When I think about it now, his call and our odd conversation were just what I should have expected from Woodard.

I haven't seen Woodard for forty-eight years, and may never see him again, but he will remain one of the most memorable characters I have ever met in my life.

Chapter 4
Parachute Jumping
A Leap of Faith

I must have been mad, I thought, to have left my buddies behind and quit the artillery unit to join the First Canadian Parachute Battalion. Since arriving in Fort Benning, Georgia, I'd undergone strenuous physical training—running, hand-to-hand combat, push-ups and other exercises—and enjoyed it all thoroughly. Somehow, I'd almost put out of my mind what the training was in preparation for—until this very moment!

Here I was, sitting in a plane with twenty-nine other apprehensive-looking soldiers—fifteen of us on each side. Each of us with a parachute strapped on our back and another on our chest. The straps that held the parachutes on were very tight, and kept pinching my groin, but that was the least of my worries. My biggest concern was whether I would have nerve enough to jump out of this plane into empty space! I knew that my question would be answered within seconds.

All eyes were on the jump-master. They had told us that he had made 250 jumps, but no one could be that foolish! He was lying on his stomach with his head sticking out the door. His hair was blowing in the wind. His job was to make sure we were over the drop zone. We'd been assured earlier that before we jumped the plane would slow down to 100 miles per hour. Big deal, I thought!

I could feel the tension as each man sat silently immersed in his own thoughts. The jump-master, however, had trained many groups of rookies, and he knew just what to do. Glancing up from his prone position, he yelled: "Is everybody happy?" A quavering voice came back to him: "Yessir." Unsatisfied, he yelled again: "Is everybody happy?" This time, a resounding "Yes! Sir!" filled the plane.

Then the jump-master started to sing the "Paratrooper's Song," which was almost shouted out, without reverence, to the tune of "The Battle Hymn of the Republic."

> Gory! gory! what a hell of a way to die!
> Gory! gory! what a hell of a way to die!
> Gory! gory! what a hell of a way to die!
> *And he ain't gonna jump no more!*

The song "celebrated" a soldier being killed on his first jump when his parachute failed to open. I, for one, wasn't inspired by such morbid bad taste, but the jump-master expected us to belt it out, so we did—at the top of our lungs!

When we'd finished the song we all fell silent, but only for a moment, because the jump-master's voice shattered the air like the crack of a whip: "Stand up! And hook up!" We stood up and lined up, single file. Then came the next order: "Equipment check!" We checked each other's equipment thoroughly. We checked the parachutes, all the straps, and especially the hook fastened to the steel cable that ran along the ceiling of the plane. The next order came all too soon: "Stand in the door!" Major Proctor, our commanding officer, was number one on the string, so he was the first man in the door. He would be the first Canadian to do a parachute jump in Fort Benning.

We all stood fidgeting, waiting for the command to jump. It seemed that everyone was pushing me, but maybe that was my imagination. Then the jump-master tapped Major Proctor on the leg and yelled: "Go!" The major jumped, and against my better instincts I followed close behind, with the others.

I closed my eyes tight as I jumped into empty space. I felt

the wind whipping around me and the sickening drop. Then I heard myself shouting: "One thousand! Two thousand!" If you reached three thousand and your main parachute didn't open you were supposed to pull the rip-cord for your emergency parachute. I didn't quite get past "Three ..." when I felt a terrific jerk, and I was practically stopped in midair! It was a bone-crushing jerk, but a wonderful sensation, to be halted in that sickening downward plunge. After flopping around, my descent settled down to a gentle swinging motion, and I was able to see the ground below me.

We had jumped from 1,200 feet. I marvelled at the view from this vantage point. The fields were not as haphazard as they appeared from the ground. I could see the patchwork of different colours in well-defined squares or rectangles. The brown, muddy Chattahoochee River wound aimlessly through the fields and disappeared beyond the horizon. Then I saw something that sent a chill up my spine. There were two ambulances parked by one of the fields. Although they looked miniature from this height, I could plainly see the Red Cross painted on the roof of each one. These were the vehicles jokingly referred to as "meat wagons." As I swung gently back and forth, I forgot about them and started to enjoy my descent in spite of myself.

The ground came up to meet me before I was quite prepared, and I hit it pretty hard. If I'd been paying better attention, I would have followed instructions better and tumbled to absorb the shock. I did tumble, but in an unintentional, awkward manner that knocked the wind out of me. Nevertheless, I was glad to have my feet back on the ground!

I gathered up my parachute and joined the others. We were loaded into trucks to return to base, and it was then that we heard the tragic news. Major Proctor, our commanding officer, had been killed! As he jumped, another plane coming behind us had struck his parachute, and he was smashed up against the plane. He died instantly. It was a very sad time for us Canadians. For some reason it numbed me rather than frightening me. I winced to think of the grisly song the jump-master had forced us to sing and the irony of it.

After five parachute jumps I was presented with my wings and issued a beautiful pair of brown jump-boots. They were high boots, unique to the Canadian Army. Before this, only officers had been permitted to wear brown shoes or boots. I spent a lot of my spare time polishing these precious boots.

My practice parachute jumps behind me, I heaved a sigh of relief. Nothing can frighten me now, I thought!

Chapter 5

Yank or Canuck?
The First Special Service Force

It was December 10, 1942, and myself and ninety-six other Canadian soldiers suddenly felt that we were facing the challenge of our lives—how to keep our identity. Not our personal identity: we all knew each other inside out, so that wasn't the issue. But we were about to lose our national identity. We had just been informed that we were now attached to the American army and would be wearing American uniforms. Here's how it happened.

x x x

Less than six months before, I had left my buddies Woodard and Beers in Tor Bay, Newfoundland, when I decided to transfer into the First Canadian Parachute Battalion. I was among the first Canadians sent to the parachute training school at Fort Benning, Georgia. (Canada, as yet, had no training facilities for sky troops.)

After we had qualified as parachutists we were marking time until facilities were completed in Camp Shilo, Manitoba, where we were to be instructors. We had nothing to do, so we spent hours everyday just marching singly, or in pairs, saluting fenceposts. We felt that we were making jackasses of ourselves in front of the Americans, and that we had been put on indefinite hold. After four months of this we wanted a change—almost any change—so when one was offered, we jumped at it!

One day we were all called out on parade, in front of a Canadian captain we'd never seen before. He introduced himself as Captain Becket and announced that he was looking

First Special Service Force colours - American Canadian Force

for volunteers for a new unit, "the Second Canadian Para-chute Battalion." He then made an irresistible offer: "I'll guar-antee the new unit will see action before this one does." I wasn't in a hurry to get killed, but when almost all of my buddies stepped forward, I felt that I had to do the same. So did most of the others, because Captain Becket got 97 volun-teers from the 127 men on parade. (Little did I know how this officer would continue to influence my army life!)

About a week later, we boarded a train and left sunny Geor-gia behind. We got off in the cold and snow of Helena, Mon-tana, and were then transported to our new base, a few miles out of town—Fort William Henry Harrison.

x x x

And that's when we learned that we had been duped. There was no Second Canadian Parachute Battalion! The unit for which we had involuntarily volunteered was an experiment—an elite group, so hush-hush that we couldn't be told about it until we got there. The "First Special Service Force," we were now informed, was a combined American-Canadian unit, only about four months old. We were to maintain Canadian discipline (King's Rules and Regulations of Canada) and continue to receive the much lower Canadian pay rate. But our first concern was our national identity. I had a fierce pride in my family, my hometown, my province, and my country. Once we put on American uniform, how long would our Canadian identity last? And the Americans, according to my prejudices, were all loud-mouthed braggarts and know-it-alls. How would they react to us? We were still wearing the uniform of the regiment we'd come from—some of us wore kilts. In the American army, all units dressed alike.

We had little time, however, to dwell on our misgivings. Here we were; there was no way out, and we immediately began training so tough that we were soon longing for our lazy days in Georgia. One of my fears—mixing with Americans—was postponed, because the Canadian volunteers were billeted separately while we were learning how to use American weapons.

We were introduced, first, to the Garand M1, a semi-automatic rifle, which could be fired repeatedly without being recocked. Its clip held eight shells; the clip ejected after the last shell was fired. The Garand was a beautiful weapon—very advanced for its time—and its inventor, after whom it was named, was a Canadian. We were proud of that, but embarrassed, too, because the Canadian Army had rejected Garand's rifle, reasoning that soldiers would have to carry so much ammunition that it would slow them down. So much for armchair generals!

The hardest thing for us to get used to about the Garand

was its sights. In the Canadian Army we'd used only open sights, whereas the Garand had a peep-sight on the back—a flat piece of metal with a pinhole in it. You looked through the hole, lined the front sight on target, and fired. We trained by firing at targets at close range and moving them back as our accuracy improved.

To my surprise, I got the hang of it pretty quickly. Our first time on the rifle range, I was beside Tommy Prince, an Indian from Manitoba, who was to become the most decorated Native soldier in the Canadian Army. "Peppard, how are you with a rifle?" Tommy asked. "Not too good," I said quickly. He held his gun as though he'd used it all his life, and I didn't want him thinking that I was competing with him! "Well," Prince said, "that's one thing I pride myself on—my ability to handle a rifle." He looked right at home as he stretched out on his stomach, spread his legs, and stabilized himself with one elbow. I tried, awkwardly, to emulate him. When the targets were collected and the scores tallied, first and second place went to guys I knew only vaguely; Tommy Prince was third—and so was I. I had tied my teacher! I was delighted, and proud, to have come third out of one hundred, but Tommy seemed a little disturbed. "I thought you said you couldn't shoot!" he said, with a mixture of anger and respect in his voice. "Well, I didn't think I could shoot that good. Maybe I was a little lucky." But I could see by the look in his eyes that Tommy Prince didn't believe in luck.

After our small-arms training, we were integrated into the outfit, and I found out quickly how misplaced my "identity crisis" and fear of Americans had been. I was put in the first company of the first regiment as a member of the 60-mm mortar crew. The other three on the crew were O'Brien, Tratt, and Smitty. O'Brien was from Connecticut, Tratt from Montreal, and Smitty—or George Smith—from faraway California. O'Brien and Smitty were as proud of their country and their hometowns as Tratt and I were of ours. The camarade-

Tommy Prince, who served in the Special Service Force, became the most decorated Native soldier in the Canadian Army.

rie that developed from learning a shared task together soon made us all best buddies.

x x x

And we remained so. O'Brien was put in charge of the mortar, and he was the soul of efficiency. He was probably seven years older than the rest of us, which in itself commanded extra respect. O'Brien and Tratt almost immediately developed a special relationship, based on their mutual love of argument. They were continually together, gnawing at bones of contention and being the best of friends.

Smitty was a small, immaculate individual. We had associated "spit and polish" with the Canadian Army, but here was an American who outshone us all! He and I, too, developed our own special bond. One night, he approached me, very confidentially. "I'm embarrassed about my body," he whispered. "What can I do to make my chest bigger?" My buddies knew that I'd lifted weights for three years before joining the army, and I had something of a reputation for my physique. So I was flattered when Smitty asked for my advice, but with no access to weights, helping him would be a challenge. I decided that we'd practise a regimen together. Every night, even after a strenuous day of training, we'd be down on the barracks-room floor doing push-ups! The rest of the guys kidded us, but after a month of puffing and sweating, Smitty proudly boasted that his chest was a half inch bigger. I was afraid to measure mine, because I was sure it had grown two inches!

x x x

I still knew little, officially, about my new unit, but the other guys in the mortar crew had joined it a few months before me, so they could answer some of my many questions. "Why is this outfit called the First Special Service Force? What's this special service we're supposed to do?" "Nobody knows," said O'Brien. "All we know is that we're going to be the best trained unit of any army in the world!" "That's a lot of malarkey!" shouted Tratt. "How do they know how the Japanese or the Germans train?" "Maybe they get it from their spies, how the hell should I know?" They told me that our training would be the best and most complete in the army, and just hearing the list exhausted me: hand-to-hand combat; demolitions; parachuting; mountain climbing; skiing; amphibious landings; and how to use a variety of weapons.

O'Brien, in particular, was proud of the claims made for our uniqueness. "We're faster, and we have a lot more firepower! We have no heavy equipment, like artillery, or tanks, so we can cover a lot of ground in a day. The sixteen men in each section carry a terrific amount of firepower! We have a Tommy Gun, a light machine gun (J.A.R.), a regular machine gun, a 60-MM mortar, a bazooka, and fifteen M1 semi-automatic rifles. There's no infantry section in the world can match that firepower!" The way O'Brien rattled off the inventory sure made it sound impressive—overwhelming even. We'd had nothing like that in the artillery unit in the Canadian Army!

I was equally curious about our chain of command, because I'd heard rumours that our C.O.—Colonel Frederick—was a mysterious, elusive figure, and something of a superman. My never having seen him gave further rein to my imagination; the truth was that I wanted even the wildest rumours to be confirmed, so as to feel that we were, indeed, "special." My buddies were eager to oblige, in fact they tried to outshout each other to be able to tell me about the colonel's bravery. What they told me was astounding; it made Colonel Frederick—for once and all—larger than life. The other guys finally subsided and let Tratt deliver the *pièce de résistance.* "The Colonel assembled us on the airfield and told us that we'd have two days of parachute training before we made our jumps. He told us that parachuting was just a small

"The greatest fighting general of all time," Winston Churchill
said of Major General Robert T. Frederick, commander of the
First Special Service Force, from July 1942 to June 1944.

part of our training. He didn't want to spend too much time on it. He said it might be just another method of reaching an objective. He said there was nothing to parachuting. Then he climbed into a plane; it took off, and a few minutes later he jumped out, and we all watched him float to the ground! And he was wearing bedroom slippers, because he'd just come out of his office! That got our respect!"

And I had to agree, for after a feat like that who wouldn't respect the man! In Fort Benning, Georgia, we had four weeks of strenuous training before we jumped for the first time.

x x x

Our training proved to be as exhaustive as promised, and in two respects the exercises were all alike: they were invigorating, and they were *frightening!* The more we trained, the more frequently I experienced, and learned to live with, what was to become my "normal" emotional state throughout the war—fear!

Amphibious training was perhaps equal parts of fear and fun. We did most of it out of Camp Bradford, near Norfolk, Virginia. We began by manipulating seven-man rubber boats on the beaches, and this brought out the little-boy-playing-by-the-seashore in all of us. Three men would straddle each side—one leg in the boat, one in the water—and paddle, while the seventh man steered, using his paddle as a tiller. We were all issued bathing trunks, and this became license for pandemonium.

Without uniforms, there was no telling a sergeant from a colonel; a corporal from a major. We ganged up on victims of our choice and threw them unceremoniously into the churning waves! Without exception, they were officers whose faces were already etched deeply into our memories. They were all forced to scramble out of the waves, sputtering and coughing, with water running from their nose and mouth! It was an enlisted man's day, and the officers were wise enough to accept it. There were too few such days!

From rubber boats, we advanced to ship-to-shore attack.

We'd board a ship, go out a mile or so from shore, scramble over the sides and scramble down rope ladders. From the ladder we'd jump into landing craft, sail to shore where the ramp would be lowered, and we'd "storm" the beaches of Chesapeake Bay with bayonets fixed and shouting like fools!

We did these exercises over and over, until they became boring to all of us. Spud Wright and I finally decided to spice things up, so we went to Norfolk and bought water pistols. The next day, Spud and I worked our way to the front of the landing craft as it approached shore, galloped down the ramp ahead of the forty or so others, then whipped the water pistols out of our belts. "Take that! and that! and that!" we shouted, as we fired spurts of water at the invisible enemy, with a plastic pistol in each hand. We turned around to see that most of our buddies were rolling around on the floor of the craft, laughing their heads off.

These ship-to-shore exercises were usually quite easy in the relatively calm waters of Chesapeake Bay, but sometimes there'd be enough of a swell that the rise and fall of the ship and the landing craft didn't work in unison. Then the exercise became frightening, because if the landing craft had fallen into a trough it became a long jump from the ladder. Weighted down with rifle, helmet and pack, you'd plummet, and crash onto the steel floor. If the landing craft was on its upward surge as the ship was sinking down, then, as you left the ladder, the floor of the landing craft would come up and meet you with a bang. I got a few bruises this way, but nothing prepared me for the Aleutians, where the gigantic ocean swells around Amchitka Island made the manoeuvre very dangerous. It was a nightmare for me to reach the bottom of the rope ladder and find that the landing craft had fallen fifteen or twenty feet lower. I had many black-and-blue marks to prove the pain of it.

There was *nothing* funny about demolitions training. A group of us stood side by side in an open field; we were given sticks of dynamite and shown how to place detonators in them with a very short fuse attached; we lit the fuse and threw the dynamite into the field. The timing was so close that, as you were lighting your fuse, a stick of dynamite would explode. At such moments I questioned my own sanity (to say nothing of that of our officers), and I wondered whether I'd even survive our training. I darkly recalled rumours about units trying to weed out "undesirables."

Our mountain-climbing instruction I found less nerve-wracking (although not all my buddies agreed with me), and I loved the cross-country skiing, which was all strength and endurance. The downhill training, though, tested my courage as much as demolitions did. When we stood at the edge of a hill and the instructor yelled, "Follow me!," my heart would leap to my throat. It wasn't too bad when the hill was bare, but a wooded hill was terrifying.

Eventually I managed to get a long rest from training altogether—but I did it the hard way. I broke my leg while trying to ski down Scratch Gravel Mountain. It was a pretty bad fracture and earned me six weeks in the base hospital.

For the first two weeks I thoroughly enjoyed the rest, the opportunity to read, the comparatively good food, and the pleasant company of the nurses. Then I began to get bored and to miss my buddies. As always during my years in the service, whenever I was sidelined I began to feel that I was missing out on something. That restlessness spurred me on to lots of adventures but often got me into trouble with the army.

When I was discharged from the hospital, I was given ten days sick leave and sent home. To be able to go home was a blessing, but it was a long, slow trip. I took a bus to Lethbridge, Alberta, and a train across Canada to Truro. That didn't leave much time to visit, so I stayed another week without leave—but that's another story!

By then I was really anxious to rejoin my unit. I began to

Mountain-climbing training in Montana. We didn't know how important our climbing skills were until we got to "La Dirensa."

Ski training, Montana, 1942. The First Special Service Force was trained to fight almost anywhere.

The author interrupts ski training for a photo opportunity—Montana, 1942.

feel somewhat guilty about my soft life, while they were training so hard. When I got back to base, my AWOL was dismissed with a reprimand, because it had taken me so long to get home. I threw myself back into army life, even though I favoured one leg for another three months.

Our unit had begun to weld itself into a highly trained and tightly knit group, and we were developing a sense that ours was indeed a "Special Force." Proudly we wore the red spearhead on our shoulder; proudly we showed the lettering on that shoulder patch—USA, CANADA.

The most important thing our training taught me was that my fears about my national identity were groundless. We all learned the same lesson. When I asked Bob Macon, from Louisiana, what the Americans had thought of us Canadians at first, he said: "We were amazed that you marched so smartly and did your precision drill." Tom Perry, from New Jersey, was less complimentary. "We thought you guys were a bunch of sissies with those skirts on, but when I lifted one of them up, I got the worst beating of my life." When the war was over, those of us who had been spared were proud to declare that we had served in a unit where, in spite of differences, we were all brothers.

First Special Service Force—parachute training, Montana, 1942.

Chapter 6
AWOL From Helena

By this time I considered myself to be a pretty fair soldier—a better than average one, even. My uniform was always pressed and neat, my shoes shined to perfection. I obeyed all orders from superiors. I never skipped a church parade. I never grumbled about the luxuries I'd given up in civilian life in order to serve my country. When I joined up, it took me two weeks of concentration, dedication, and hard work to graduate from the "awkward squad." I did it by practising rifle drill alone in the barracks at night, while others played cards, went on pass, listened to the radio, or wrote letters home. I was determined to make a success of this soldier bit. I was fiercely patriotic and believed that if King George the Sixth weren't God Himself, he was a very short step down the ladder from Him!

However, I discovered, during the course of more than four years in the army, that I had one almost unforgivable—potentially fatal flaw as a soldier: I was given to breaking military law, periodically, by being absent without leave. "Going AWOL," as it was called, is a military crime, and depending upon the circumstances it may be treated as a very serious one. I went AWOL five times—as I recall—and the circumstances varied; from leaving training camp without a proper pass and overstaying a leave, to taking an extended vacation from a theatre of war, which is sometimes considered desertion—a serious crime indeed. Only once was my punishment very severe, although once, but for the grace of God and my fleet feet, I might have been shot! And, of course, I had no idea the first time I went AWOL that I was starting a habit.

It seemed to be an act of spontaneous collective stupidity, but the catalyst was that my buddies and I suddenly became rich—relatively speaking. Many of us had transferred into the First Canadian Parachute Battalion at the same time, shared our growing disillusionment with that outfit, and stepped forward together on the parade square when Captain Becket had asked for volunteers for a unit that didn't exist. All of that "togetherness" had two results: one was the effect upon the military bureaucracy, which couldn't keep track of our moving around; so for a long time our paybooks, documents, and papers didn't reach us, and we didn't get paid; the second effect was—not surprisingly—on us. So much moving around, frustration, readjustment, topped off by the superhuman rigours of our training in the Special Services Force, meant that we had all built up a pretty good head of steam.

One day, after we'd been in our new unit for about a month and a half, our back pay caught up with us. Mine came to $123.80—about the same as for everyone who'd come from Georgia. That was a windfall, since we made about $47.00 per month. We were stunned. For a very short time each of us pondered, privately, on how we could spend it all at once; and then I heard Spud Wright whisper to another Canadian, Andy Billan: "We're goin' home!" And that was my answer!

I still don't know who came up with the idea, but for some of us it opened the valves so we could let off all of that accumulated steam. Before long, seventeen of us were hunkered together at the end of the barracks planning our getaway. It was just like in the movies, when James Cagney and his prison buddies schemed to break out of the "big house." Andy Billan had the best penmanship, so he wrote out the passes, (which had been stolen from the orderly room). Spud Wright signed them all with an almost reverent flourish: "Captain Davidson

J.N." Spud assured us that the good captain was the terror of the Third Regiment, but I still don't know whether he even existed.

Not for a moment did I question the feasibility of our plan, even though Nova Scotia lay some thirty-five hundred miles away. None of us questioned it; and before long we were all sitting aboard the bus at Helena, excited, and then elated as it pulled away while two military police stood in the terminal, completely oblivious to the escaping criminals.

It was nine o'clock on a bitterly cold January evening. We escapers were the majority of the passengers. We kept looking uneasily back towards the town, expecting to see about ten jeeps, loaded with MPs, roaring after us, but as the lights faded in the distance we all relaxed. Everyone began smiling and joking. Spud Wright, struck up his favourite song: "Jeannie, the Queenie of the Burlesque Show," and once we'd made sure that all the rest of the travellers were men, we launched into our repertoire of ribald army songs. Bunched together at the back of the bus, we sang our hearts out: songs like "Roll Me Over in the Clover," "The Gathering of the Clan," "The Old Monk," "When There Isn't a Girl About," and many, many more—some of them coarse even by army standards. When we'd about exhausted ourselves and were just settling back to rest, someone pulled the bell cord. When the bus stopped, a man in front got up, took down his bag, then turned and gave us all a prolonged look of disapproval bordering on disgust. It was only then that I saw his clerical collar! My God! I slouched down to avoid those condemning eyes, but I knew he was looking directly at me. What a relief when he eventually stepped down and disappeared into the night.

We travelled all night. Come dawn we approached a town. Through the frosty windows, I saw a sign: Shelby, Montana. Pop. 11,101. Pete Cottingham yelled: "We're only fifty miles from the Alberta border!" We'd soon be in Canada, I thought, and then I'd just board the CNR train and head straight for good old Truro, Nova Scotia.

The bus stopped in front of a large, grey, masonry building, and a man wearing a Mackinaw jacket, and the inevitable big cowboy hat, got on and talked with the driver. The driver turned to us and said, "All you soldier boys get out with your luggage." Some of us were alarmed by this, but Andy Billan reassured us that it was "Customs,"—just a baggage check before we crossed the border. We happily piled out, carrying haversacks. I was in front, and I trustingly followed the big hat and Mackinaw jacket right into the imposing looking building.

As soon as I walked through the doorway, I realized the truth. There were bars everywhere I looked, and one huge cell had its door ajar, in a most inviting manner. Besides the man in the Stetson, (We later learned he was the sheriff), there were five other purposeful looking men. Each of them cradled a shotgun in the crook of his arm. I nearly panicked then and considered turning around and trying to escape, but that would have been futile because sixteen onrushing, unthinking soldiers were propelling me forward. They were anxious to get this formality over with, so that they could proceed on their "leave." Slowly, but inevitably, I was pushed into the "welcoming" cell where I was soon joined by the rest of our crew, after a little persuasion from the kindly gentlemen with the shotguns.

So there we were, looking out through the bars, our dreams of going home shattered. For a few moments we just milled around, bumping into each other like cattle, still not quite sure what had happened. The sheriff got right on the phone, and his message soon brought us back to the here and now.

"Let me have the army camp at Fort William Henry Harrison in Helena, will you?" After a little wait, he said: "We got them—seventeen of them. Yes. Tomorrow? OK."

COUNTY OF TOOLE

JOHN BROOKS,
Sheriff
Phone: 434-5358

WILLIAM CADY,
Undersheriff
Phone: 434-2844

DABELL CADY,
Deputy
Phone: 434-2818

CLARE KIMBALL,
Deputy
Phone: 937-3311

Office of Sheriff John Brooks
PHONE 434-5588
Shelby, Montana 59474

21 August 1972

Attention: Survivors of the 'Club'

On returning to Canada from the Force reunion in Helena last week my family and I were passing through Shelby, Montana. Recalling our experience in that town of nearly thirty years ago I decided to drive around and see if we could find the old hoosgow. Sure enough the old building is still there and is still being used as "Crow-Bar Hotel".

Sheriff John Brooks was kind enough to show us through the place and even took us upstairs to see the "tank" we all occupied. It hasn't changed a bit – just the inmates.

I asked him if the records would show the names of the seventeen of us who were "guests" there so long ago. He turned the pages way back in his big ledger and there, under the date of January 17th, 1943 the following names were listed:

ASHLEY, J.
PEPPARD, G. H.
BILLAN, A.
BROTHERTON, W.
BALDWIN, Q.
STOYCHEFF, J. B.
LaBOUCHILLER, L.
HARRY, W. B.
COTTINGHAM, P. L.

RUSCONI, G.
WRIGHT, G. W.
ZIMMERMAN, W. A.
LIPSCOMBE, R.
PARE, L.
WRIGHT, A. L.
LITSTER, C.
LUECK, J.

Of the above listed men I have personal knowledge that W. Brotherton and W. B. Harry were killed in action. Of the remainder several are known to me and it gives me pleasure to mail a copy of this letter to those whose addresses are known.

Sincerely,

Peter L. Cottingham

Peter L. Cottingham
Box 596 Neepawa, Manitoba

P.S. This 'hotel' stationery was supplied courtesy of Sherriff Brooks.

AWOL! Seventeen Canadians decided to go home when we got our back pay. Andy Billan signed all the passes. We only got as far as Shelby, Montana.

Short and to the point. Turning from the phone, he told us to relax, because the MPs wouldn't be up for us till next day.

Our stupidity began to sink in, and we might have all become exceedingly miserable, but our "hosts" were so friendly that we soon resigned ourselves and then began to feel better. Being young and adaptable, we did the only sensible thing under the circumstances: we tried to make ourselves comfortable. Food was passed in to us, and we were all given mattresses. Before long we were talking, joking, and playing cards. We accepted that the sheriff and his deputies were just doing their jobs, and they certainly didn't treat us like hardened criminals.

As the sheriff came over to our cell, he drawled, "Boys, I've been talking with the mayor, and a few of the town council. They've come up with a proposal to put before you. We see very few soldiers in this town, and the only thing we seem to do for the war effort is buy bonds and collect scrap. Now, we feel at last we can do something tangible. We'd like you soldiers to be guests of the town of Shelby. You can go the movies—under guard of course—eat at our restaurants, and drink at the bars, all free, gratis, and all compliments of our town. But this hinges on one condition: you must give your word you will not try to escape!" We were nearly bowled over. The goodwill and generosity of this little town went a long way towards restoring our good spirits.

So the non-drinkers—eight of us—headed for a restaurant, where we were waited on very courteously by a beautiful waitress. I basked in her beauty and the warm surroundings just as long as I possibly could, but after a steak and onions, three coffees, and four large pieces of apple pie, I felt that I was overstaying my welcome.

Then we all went and joined the rest of the boys at the barroom. I'd never been in a drinking establishment before, and I was very impressed. The large shiny bar, with a brass footrail and the bartender, looking like a fancy doorman in his bow-tie seemed very elegant indeed. I'll always remember the life-size painting that hung behind the bar. It depicted two boxers—Jack Dempsey and Gibbons—slugging it out. We were told that they had fought in this very town in 1920. Dempsey, of course, was the winner, with Gibbons going out the way of most of Jack's opponents—feet first. Those of us who didn't drink decided to go to a movie. I've forgotten the film, but I remember that we attracted a lot of attention, which seemed very flattering, until I remembered that there was an armed deputy standing at each door. After the movie—well fed, and well entertained—we returned to our cell. About two hours later, the boys we had left at the bar came back in a very jovial mood.

About 8:30 the next morning, in strode ten MPs, armed to the teeth and prepared for any eventuality. They needn't have worried: our fantasy of going home was already history to

49

us. We had been buffered and bolstered by the friendliness of Shelby, so we were docile—even a bit sheepish.

On the way back to camp, in an army truck, my critical faculties finally started to function. How naive we'd been! It wouldn't have taken long to discover our absence from camp: there was a roll call at 6:30 every morning. Our superiors knew that we were all Canadians; there was only one road to the border and it passed right through Shelby. It was just a matter of phoning the sheriff there and telling him the expected time of arrival of seventeen very dumb criminals.

We weren't punished very severely, maybe because our escapade was so poorly planned that it was considered childish rather than serious. I suppose I was hit the hardest: I lost my corporal's stripes and the little bit of extra pay they earned me, whereas the privates were only confined to base, I don't remember for how long.

I must have thought at that moment that I'd never go AWOL again. Why would I want to repeat such a disaster? Indeed, I never planned my absences long in advance; they were always spur-of-the-moment decisions, overwhelming urges. I still don't know, rationally, why I so frequently risked demotion, humiliation, and imprisonment for a few days away from army routine. I know that I sometimes resented the limitations army life put on my individuality. Maybe I felt I was different from the rest of the young men who endured so much regimentation. Maybe I resented the orders from corporals, sergeants, and officers. Everybody seemed to be my superior. Maybe I just got damned tired of lining up for roll call, for church, for pay, for inspection, for guard duty—for everything! There came a time when I felt that I just had to get away and do as I wished. But I think most of the men felt similar emotions; the difference was that they never acted on them, whereas I had to. There was something in me of my headstrong buddy Woodard from my old artillery unit. That was what I had liked about him.

More importantly, my AWOLs gave me a sense of adventure that I could only experience on my own, and they changed my life. It was while I was absent without leave that I met Greta, the girl of my dreams!

I've often felt some guilt about my flaw as a soldier, some sense of letting down my superiors, who had such confidence in me. But whenever I ask myself whether I'd go AWOL if I had it to do over again, the answer is always—of course—a resounding yes!

Chapter 7

Everything's Coming Up Roses
Meeting Greta

I went AWOL again in September 1943, and what a blessed decision that proved to be, because the most important, most glorious day of my life occurred while I was back home in Truro, Nova Scotia!

x x x

It was a beautiful late summer's day. I was twenty-three years old, and I was strolling happily down Prince Street, wearing my paratrooper uniform—with a well-pressed jacket and pants, and shiny high brown jump-boots—and licking a double-header ice-cream cone.

I had just passed the Royal Bank, and was approaching Thomas's Book Store when I heard a voice calling from across the street. I looked over toward the Maritime Tel & Tel Office and coming across the street was the most beautiful girl I'd ever seen! I almost looked around, to see who was the lucky person she was talking to, but I knew that there was no one else nearby. Across the street she came, and I was certain I'd never seen her before, because if I had I'd never have forgotten.

"Do you know my brother, Mosher MacPhee?" she asked. "He's in your unit, isn't he?" Mosher and I had trained together in Fort Benning, Georgia, at the paratrooper training camp, before I had transferred into the First Special Service Force. We talked a little about Mosher, but all the while I was fascinated with his lovely sister, who introduced herself as "Greta." I strove my utmost to appear nonchalant, but my heart was thumping so hard that I thought she would see it

through my jacket. For all of my travelling, I was still anything but worldly wise. In fact, I was quite naive, innocent,
and bashful around girls. I guess that's why I tried so hard to
impress Greta with my cleverness, and to seem blasé—as
though having beautiful girls call out to me and wish to talk
with me were an everyday occurrence. Gazing at her gorgeous face, I blurted out: "How did you get your lipstick on
so straight?"

How often I wished, later, that I could have swallowed
those words. But the moment passed without Greta making
a big thing of it, and the longer we talked, the more comfortable I felt—and the more my ice cream melted over my hand.

x x x

My entire visit home was a very special one. I had a wonderful reunion with my parents and my eight brothers and sisters, in our family home. Ours is a close-knit family, with
great traditions and memories to bind us together. However,
I have to repeat that the high point—the miracle—of my visit
was meeting Greta. Nothing could make me feel bad after
that, not even the fact that I was now in deep trouble with
the army.

I got back to camp at midnight, September 21, 1943, after
being absent without leave for eleven days, and I'd no sooner
stepped into the barracks than I was confronted by our sergeant-major. "Be ready to be paraded before the battalion
commander first thing tomorrow morning!" he barked. "You
really stepped out of line this time!"

Let me say in my own, admittedly weak, defence, that I
had some pretty good excuses for going AWOL this time.
Our unit was temporarily stationed at Fort Ethan Allen, Ver-
mont—tantalizingly close to Nova Scotia—but rumour was
that we were soon to be posted overseas. Half the unit had
been given immediate leave—which seemed to corroborate
the rumour—but I wasn't among the fortunate ones. I began
to worry that I'd be posted overseas without leave, and I

couldn't take that chance, so I decided to break army law yet again. After four days at home, however, I became afraid that my unit might leave without me, so I sent a telegram to my platoon commander, Lieutenant Gray. Jim O'Brien told me later that he was in the orderly room when my message arrived and Lieutenant Gray read it aloud: "I am at my home, will be back September 21st." The lieutenant, Jim said, exploded: "Who the hell does he think he is!" My gesture had obviously not had the desired effect, and the fact that I was as good as my word didn't impress my superiors.

The next morning the sergeant-major marched me into Major Becket's office. (Yes, the good captain, who had recruited me for the Special Services Force had been promoted and was now my battalion commander.) It was all cut-and-dried for the sergeant-major. I was just another offender who had broken the law found in that big army book lying on the major's desk. The book, which was abbreviated to "K.R. of Can.," was officially titled "King's Rules of Canada."

I can still hear the staccato commands of the sergeant-major: "Left, right! Left, right! Left, right!" The commands came so fast that I thought he must be in a great hurry, but maybe he was just trying to show his superior how efficient he was.

I stood stiffly at attention in front of Major Becket. I thought it strange that he should look so very angry. Was he taking all this personally? It had nothing to do with him. All he had to do was sentence me, and I'd be out of his hair. Instead, he sat there staring at me. His face was beet-red. His eyes, through the extra-thick lenses of his glasses, looked three times their regular size. I wondered how he'd gotten into the Canadian Army with such poor vision. Then I remembered that he'd been a lawyer in civilian life. With so much education, I reasoned, the army could overlook some minor physical defect.

When, finally, he vented his feelings, I realized that he had some justification for being upset. As he yelled at me, I be-

*Lieutenant Colonel R.W. (Bill) Becket—Italy, 1944—C.O. of
Third Regiment, Special Service Force. As Captain he recruited
volunteers (including Herb Peppard) for the force; as a Major he
sentenced Herb for going AWOL.*

gan to feel a little remorse. "It seems to me, Peppard, that you soldier when you want to, and take a leave whenever you want to!" That was a true statement, I thought. Although I trained hard and usually obeyed orders conscientiously, I already had two AWOL charges against me. So I stood stiffly at attention awaiting my major's sentence. "I'm going to hit you where it hurts the most, soldier—right in the pocketbook! Twenty-eight days detention and twenty-eight days automatic forfeiture of pay! March him out!"

On an order from the sergeant-major, it was: "Right turn! Quick march! Left, right! Left, right!" But before I'd reached the door the major let out a bellow: "Hold it there! March him back in!" A change of heart, I wondered. Would he lighten the sentence, or have me executed? But the major, true to form, was just following the rules—to a T. He had overlooked a minor clause that was nestled in his precious law book. "Do you accept my punishment?" he asked, in a manner that admitted but one answer: "Yes, sir!" I replied crisply.

Then I was marched out, under guard, taken to my barracks and ordered to collect the things that I would need during my twenty-eight days in jail. My buddies—Tratt, O'Brien, Smitty—crowded around me as I was collecting my shaving gear, towel, socks, and underwear. "What did he give you, Pep?" O'Brien asked. "Twenty-eight days in the guardhouse." "The pompous son of a bitch!" exclaimed Smitty. The others muttered agreement.

AWOL, while looked upon as a serious crime by the army, was seen very differently by the common soldier. A person could stand just so much regimentation, so many orders, so many restrictions. After a certain point, if he didn't get a leave, he just took off. Those were my sentiments, and because of what everyone considered a stiff sentence, I had the sympathy of the entire platoon.

Not that I was depressed. I was still riding high on my thoughts of Greta and my family, and I hadn't expected, af-

ter all, to be officially congratulated for going AWOL—so I was prepared for my punishment.

Two military police, carrying shotguns, escorted me to the guardhouse. I was hustled into a cell with five other men. As I looked at the cell, the armed guards, and my cellmates, I began to feel that I must indeed be a criminal. But the other inmates gave me a friendly welcome to my temporary home, and I soon decided to make the best of it, having no sensible alternative.

There were many cells—all similar. The wall that contained the door was bars from floor to ceiling. One other wall was all bars, while the other two were outside walls, one with a small barred window that was too high to see out of. The cell was about twenty feet square. There were three two-tier bunks standing by the walls. A rough table surrounded by four chairs occupied the centre of the cell.

Suddenly a bell rang, and one of the guys grunted, "chow time." A guard opened the cell door and led us to the mess hall. There must have been thirty-five or forty of us gathered there for supper, and the food was surprisingly good. But even if it had been as bad as I expected, I wouldn't have complained, because the four guards standing around the walls holding shotguns, weren't smiling. I didn't think that anyone should provoke them.

I noticed that I was getting some stares, and I felt nervous until it dawned on me that I was still dressed in army pants and a shirt, while they all wore olive-green coveralls with a big white *P* on the back. They were simply looking at the newcomer, who would soon be wearing the same "uniform" as them.

As soon as we were ushered back to our cells, I climbed onto my bunk and stretched out to relax. Suddenly, our door was flung open with a loud clank, and there stood my old friend, the sergeant-major. "OK, let's get at it!" he shouted. He threw me my prisoner's coveralls, then I joined the others for the evening ritual. First, we went into a storeroom and each picked up a backpack, helmet, and a rifle. The backpack only weighed about forty pounds, but I knew that it would soon feel much heavier. The rifle, a standard M1 army issue, had neither bayonet nor ammunition—of course.

Then it was out to the parade square where we were marched from one end to the other, continuously, for the next three hours. By the third hour, my pack felt like it weighed one hundred pounds. Because I was sweating a lot, the straps started to chafe my shoulders. The sergeant-major seemed to be enjoying every minute of our torture, and some of the men began muttering bitter obscenities about him but I vowed to endure silently. I had a fierce pride that would keep me going even if my body failed me. I told myself that I would do this three-hour pack drill every night of my confinement if necessary! I soon found out that my vow would be tested to the utmost.

Our days were more pleasant. Work was voluntary, but I didn't want to lie around a prison cell all day. Three of us—with our personal armed guard close behind—had the task of gathering the camp's garbage. To collect it, we were given the use of a mule and wagon. Fort Ethan Allen was a large camp that had been a permanent army base. It boasted a tennis court, a theatre, and some houses. Besides our unit of 2,500 men, it housed soldiers from other units. There were also quite a number of army women—nicknamed WACs, from the initials of their official name, Women's Army Corps.

Apart from the slop from the kitchen, collecting garbage wasn't too bad a job. We especially enjoyed getting into the WACs' trash cans, where we'd dig out letters from their boyfriends. As we read their promises of undying love and devotion, we would joke around and argue over how many of these protestations were serious. There were millions of such letters going to all parts of the globe, and if all the separated lovers were as lonely as these ones, it must be a sad, sad world! I thought of Greta, and I wanted to write her happy letters.

We had just finished supper one night, and were getting saddled up for our pack drill, when I received a visitor. "I'll give you two minutes," growled the sergeant-major. "This ain't no Sunday School picnic, ya know! We got some marchin' to do!" My two-minute guest was George Wright, a buddy from the unit and a happy-go-lucky fellow who must have come to cheer me up. But he looked uncharacteristically downcast and sheepish, and he started making small talk, so that I had to remind him of the sergeant-major's time limit. George stared at the floor and got to the point of his visit, adopting an apologetic tone: "Pep, I've been going out with your girlfriend in Burlington."

I was taken aback. I didn't know what to say, or how to

Me (with dog) and my buddy George Wright who visited me in jail, did me a great favour and is a friend to this day!

react. I suppose that I should have been offended, but I wasn't. I guess I should have appreciated George's awkward attempt at honesty—and I guess I did. But the truth was that I didn't care that much: my thoughts were all for Greta, and in a way he'd done me a favour, although he didn't know that, and I certainly wasn't about to tell him.

I shrugged, as if to say, "Thanks for being man enough to tell me, George. If she prefers you, what can I say but 'Good luck.' " I don't remember exactly what I did say to him, but it must have been the right thing, because he smiled and his spirits picked up. He left, relieved that an awkward situation had been resolved. (Our friendship continued and does to this day. Oddly enough, George has forgotten the incident. All I can say is, "Gee, George, thanks for coming to cheer me up!")

x x x

One Saturday night, after pack drill, the head guard asked: "Anyone want to go to the movie?" "Can we change out of these coveralls?" we asked. "No. That's the catch. You either go as a group, in your prison clothes, or you don't go at all." Some of the men declined, because they were ashamed to be seen in prison garb, but I was eager to go. Very few people in camp knew me anyway, and it would be no surprise to my buddies. So nine of us were marched to the theatre by two guards. We sat in a group, looking, I imagine, just like a bunch of jailbirds—and we got more attention than the movie, at least from some of the kids and their mothers. I've long since forgotten what the film was, but I often wonder whether those soldiers' families thought that we were hard-core criminals, and what the mothers told their kids about us. It was kind of neat to steal the show—and it sure broke the monotony of prison life!

It was a happy day when my sentence ended, although I can't say that I suffered much in the guardhouse—except from boredom and the sergeant-major's nightly attempts to make me collapse from exhaustion and beg for mercy. (He didn't know that I had a secret weapon to sustain me—my thoughts of Greta.) Experiencing confinement gave me a different perspective on freedom. I returned enthusiastically to army life, where you do what you're ordered to do; you get up when you're told, train when you're told, eat when you're told, go to bed when you're told, go to foreign lands when you're told, and fight to the death when you're told! Freedom is, indeed, a relative thing. Philosophy aside, my first day out was like a breath of fresh air. I got to see my buddies; I could go for a meal without having an armed escort; I could get a pass to the nearby town of Burlington and shop in the stores or eat in a restaurant. (Of course, thanks to Major Becket's sentence, I had almost no money to spend, and the girl I'd been seeing in town was now going out with my friend George.)

Soon after, my unit was posted overseas, and I didn't see Greta again until I returned from overseas almost two years later.

Would I have gotten a pass home before we went into action? I don't know. But I know that I did the right thing for me. Later, when I discovered Robert Frost's poem "The Road Not Taken," I appreciated even more the importance of my decision—and of a chance meeting. If I'd walked down Queen Street instead of Prince Street that day in Truro, would I ever have met Greta MacPhee? What would have sustained me through the hard years of the war?

Thank you, God, and thanks to fate. And thank you, Colonel Becket (Yes, he kept on being promoted), and thank you, George. In some round-about way everything came up roses for me. I married my gorgeous girl after the war; we have three wonderful children and seven beautiful grandchildren, and our love and faithfulness lasted forty-six precious years.

And I'll never forget Prince Street—a warm summer day, ice cream, and a melodious female voice calling: "Hey, soldier!"

Chapter 8
The Aleutian Islands

"Kiska? Never heard of the place!" roared Bradley. Our commanding officer, Colonel Frederick, had just announced, over the ship's loudspeaker, that this unknown place was our objective. It was an island held by the Japanese. It had to be taken, and the First Special Service Force was to lead the assault. After all our training, this was to be our first test in combat. Only the day before (August 11, 1943) we had sailed out under the Golden Gate Bridge—destination unknown. I had waved farewell to a lone couple who were strolling hand in hand along the bridge. I guess the colonel felt that it was safe to tell us now, because there was no way the news could leak out.

"Where the hell is this Kiska, anyway?" grumbled Bradley. "It sounds like a damn Russian name to me!" Someone knew that it was one of the Aleutian Islands, and we knew, roughly, that they were a string of islands in the Bering Sea, starting at Alaska and stretching out towards Japan. During our voyage, we were given maps and briefed on our objective. The islands of Attu and Kiska—those closest to Japan—had been occupied by the Japanese. This had greatly disturbed both Canada and the United States. Therefore, these two islands must be taken.

Soon we heard some good news, and some bad news. The good news was that the Americans had taken Attu, the outermost island. The bad news was that only 31 of the 2,300 Japanese defending the island had been taken prisoner. The rest had either fought to the death or committed suicide! I was shocked and incredulous. What kind of people would be fighting? Death seemed to hold no terror for them. In fact, it seemed that they welcomed it. This was against all my principles. My main object in life was to stay alive. My morale plummeted at the news.

Not only did I think that I was sailing into the teeth of death, but the voyage itself—on the S.S. *Nathaniel Wyeth* was a nightmare. These "Liberty ships," as they were known, had been built amazingly quick by Kaiser, the automobile manufacturer, and they were not built for comfort. They not only plunged up and down, fore and aft, but they rolled from side to side. I'm not a very seaworthy person, so I was sick for most of the thirteen-day voyage.

I had been very determined not to get seasick. I had been told that as long as I kept eating I would be all right. With this good advice in mind, I staggered along the rolling deck to the mess hall. I descended the narrow stairs to the huge dining room. I saw the giant table, with bowls, cups, and plates sliding around the table top with each roll of the ship. I kept saying to myself, "Don't give in, don't give in!" Then I saw one fellow turn a sickly greenish colour, rock forward, and throw up in his bowl of food. That finished me. I staggered back to my bunk, where I spent most of the rest of the trip.

One sunny morning I forced myself to venture out on deck for a breath of fresh air. The first thing I saw was a crowd gathered in a big circle. They were all staring at a huge bucket that was turned upside down on the deck. I heard one of them whisper something about a flying fish. Then one of the guys yelled to me, "Have you ever seen a flying fish?" I hadn't, and up until then, I had doubted that they existed. I was overwhelmingly curious, so I walked over to the bucket. A voice in the crowd advised: "Just lift it slowly, and not too far. We don't want to lose him." There was nothing there. Before I could turn around, I was delivered a terrific whack across my backside that sent me staggering. When I recovered, I saw my buddy, Bradley, holding a big board. Everyone was laughing uproariously. I had been the butt, so to speak, of an elaborate joke—a prank to relieve the boredom of the long ocean voyage. My anger dissipated when I was handed the board and given the chance to paddle some other naive, unsuspecting landlubber. And I did!

Our convoy picked up more ships as it approached Vancouver. The assault on Kiska was to be a joint Canadian and American operation. Our combined task force numbered 30,000. The Japanese on Kiska were estimated at 11,000; however, if the enemy always fought to the death, we would need our superior numbers.

I soon returned to my rocking and rolling bunk. Tratt, the lucky devil, never got seasick, and he'd bring me food from the mess hall. I couldn't take anything greasy, so he brought oranges and bread, which my stomach accepted grudgingly.

One day we received a radio broadcast over the loudspeaker. It was propaganda from Tokyo. The beautiful female voice was none other than the infamous "Tokyo Rose." I can't recall what she said, but it fascinated me, in a spooky way, to hear the enemy speaking English.

On July 22, we arrived at the island of Adak. Our ship anchored inside the submarine net. It was very foggy, and what little we could see was not encouraging. Whenever the fog lifted, we saw a stark, bare, hostile-looking environment. There were no trees and not even bushes. The ground was covered with mossy grass. With a break in the fog, a couple of huge mountains loomed up. The whole place looked very weird and out of this world.

We thought we'd be debarking here, but the big brass had other ideas. We weighed anchor and put to sea again. A day later, we arrived at the island of Amchitka. This was to be our home for the next month. We pitched tents and dug foxholes. Many of us were pressed into unloading the supplies, and some guys buried as many boxes of food as they could in the muskeg, against future need. But this hoarding left the more honest—or cautious—of us, short of rations. We said nothing to our officers, of course. That would have been squealing.

Hunger pangs drove Tratt, Smitty, O'Brien, and me down to the ocean to fish. We were ill-equipped, but determined. We bent pins for hooks and found something for bait. I pulled in the first fish, but it was such a scary-looking thing that I instantly hurled it back into the cold waters of the Bering Sea! It was about a foot and a half long, with a huge head— out of all proportion to the rest of its body—and great, long whiskers. For me, a fish was the beautiful pink trout that we pulled out of the streams of Nova Scotia. The monstrous creature made me further doubt that this forbidding land was part of our planet.

But we were too hungry to give up, and Smitty and O'Brien each caught a more palatable-looking specimen. We took them back to the tent and built a fire. Because we had no cooking pot, we boiled the fish in a helmet. I think that something burned off our makeshift pot and added its "flavour" to our stew. It sure didn't taste like Mum's cooking, but we ate it anyway.

A few days later our field kitchen was set up, and we were introduced to powdered milk and powdered eggs. We'd rather not have met them, since they didn't compare with the real thing, but like our fish stew, they were better than nothing.

In training, we tried something new, to improve our efficiency. The mortar crew, it seemed, always had too much to carry—rifle, ammunition, helmet, pack, along with mortar bombs and mortar parts. Our 60-mm mortar had a separate steel base-plate that was very heavy. Our officers showed us a captured Japanese mortar; it had no detachable base-plate. A semi-circular piece of metal fastened to the bottom of the

barrel served the same function and was much lighter. The allies called the Japanese mortar a "knee-mortar." We were told that the U.S. Marines had taken the name to heart, and had decided to experiment using a captured Japanese mortar. A marine had knelt down and placed the semi-circular base on his thigh, but when the mortar was fired, the recoil was so powerful that it broke his leg. If we hadn't heard this story, I'm sure some damn fool in our outfit would have tried the same trick.

The possibility of not having to carry the burdensome baseplate inspired Captain Gray. "Why not use a helmet as a baseplate for the mortar?" he asked. Well, a suggestion from an officer was almost an order, and who were we to question a superior's idea! I readily volunteered my helmet, after removing the lining. A shell was dropped down the barrel of the mortar; the mortar fired; the bomb flew out the barrel.

Everything worked perfectly, except for one slight detail. The recoil drove the base of the mortar right through my helmet! Captain Gray had to admit defeat, and we continued to lug the heavy base-plate.

It was on Amchitka that we first tried out a new American army weapon—the Johnson automatic rifle—and I overheard Major Becket say disdainfully to another Canadian officer, "It's a mighty fine weapon, but it's *not a Bren!*" The Bren gun was standard issue in the British and Canadian Armies.

Bombers regularly took off from Amchitka to bomb Kiska. For the first time, I saw the American P-38, a sleek plane with a twin fuselage. "They'll never get any better than this!" I said to myself. Before the end of the war, of course, the jet had been developed, and it made even the P-38 seem primitive.

Most of our nights were spent in our tent, reading poetry to each other. That may seem to be a strange activity for us "rough and tough" soldiers, but I had enjoyed poetry all my life, and I had brought some of my favourite poets with me. The days were long up in the Aleutians. It was daylight till about 11:30 at night, which made it hard to sleep. I started to convert some of the "non-believers," and we passed the time talking and reading poetry. I had brought books by Robert Service, Pauline Johnson, and Edgar Allan Poe. Our favourites were "The Raven," and "Fleurette." We spent many happy hours with these poets.

One night I was given sentry duty on the beach. It was very dark and I couldn't see much, but I continually looked out to sea. I could envision a horde of Japanese wading in towards the shore, waving those big samurai swords, all descending on the lonesome figure shivering there—*me!*

We were only sixty miles from Kiska, but we were forbidden ammunition while on guard duty. I couldn't understand the thinking of our superiors. What we were supposed to do if we encountered the enemy, I had no idea. Maybe the officers thought that we'd be so edgy that we'd shoot our own men. Whatever the reason, we guarded the barren beaches with empty rifles.

Then the high command had another brainstorm. They decided to test our endurance, our stamina, our discipline, and our morale. They ordered a twenty-four hour route march—full pack! We had done many route marches, but not on terrain like this. We started the march one rainy, foggy morning at 9:00 A.M. With every step we sank into the wet spongy muskeg, and before long, our legs felt like jelly. Every hour, we were given a ten-minute break and we stopped for an hour at midnight. The rain took no breaks, but that was almost a blessing—if it hadn't been for the terrible weather, I'm sure that we would all have fallen asleep on our feet. We arrived back at camp at 2:00 P.M.—the elements had stretched our ordeal to twenty-nine hours. We had quite a few casualties; one of them was our section leader, Staff-Sergeant Airth. The insides of his thighs were like raw meat. When his rough pants had gotten wet, they'd chafed his legs so badly that they'd worn the skin right off. He'd endured a lot of pain to finish the march, but he'd gained a lot of respect from his men. Within a few weeks he was given a field promotion to lieutenant, and we all felt that he deserved it.

There were many units stationed on Amchitka, and its facilities even included a theatre. One evening I went to see a movie. The only thing that I remember about the occasion is the screaming, whistling, and groaning that erupted whenever a girl appeared on the screen. This startled and alarmed me, but I understood their behaviour better when I learned that some of these men had been up here for two-and-a-half years.

On August 14, we embarked for Kiska aboard a landing ship tank (LST), a ship designed to carry tanks. On this occasion, however, it was loaded with seven-man rubber boats, so that we could land as quietly as possible. The front of the ship had a ramp, down which we were to drag our landing craft into the water. This was to be our first combat, and, in my imagination, the enemy awaiting us was almost super-human. Small wonder that I was terrified as we sailed into the unknown!

Ships loading for the assult on the Island of Kiska.

Chapter 9
Kiska

Our ship stopped about three-quarters of a mile from Kiska. It was nearly midnight when we were ordered to "saddle up" and get ready to move out. I guess this was when it sunk in that we were real soldiers now—that many of us might soon be dead. For the first time, we also felt a real sense of comradeship and mutual dependency. A lot of us went around the huge open shell of the ship, shaking hands and wishing each other well.

The huge ramp lowered slowly, creaking all the way, announcing our presence like an alarm signal piercing the surrounding silence. We were ordered to get our rubber boats into the water quickly. As we dragged them along the ship's floor they rolled over empty ration cans we had tossed there. This set up a clattering that I was sure could be heard by every Japanese as far away as Tokyo.

It took a long time to get all of the boats into the water, and almost immediately there was a near tragedy. One of the men—MacIver—lost his balance and tumbled into the frigid Bering Sea. Lieutenant Airth quickly ordered his crew to row back, and they pulled him to safety. The lieutenant's decision was a direct violation of an absolute order; under no circumstances was our convoy to break ranks. Had he been called up on it, Lieutenant Airth might have been subject to the most severe military discipline; but had humanity not overruled orders, we would undoubtedly have suffered our first casualty. MacIver, half frozen, was grateful, to say the least. We rejoined the rest of the force quickly, and we all rowed around in a big circle until all the landing craft were clear of the ship. Then we paddled, single file, behind our company commander towards the shore. He had a huge phosphorescent "1" stuck on the back of his boat, so that the First Company could follow him to shore.

Our progress towards shore was painfully slow. The tide was against us, and we were carrying full packs and weapons. This strange sea now took on an eerie dimension, because every time a paddle was pulled through the water, it gave off a phosphorescent light. We felt that thousands of eyes could see our every move. We could just make out the dark silhouette of the shoreline, which seemed to come no closer. Suddenly, the silence was shattered. Without warning, huge navy guns opened up, blasting the island. The ships were about three miles offshore, and we could hear the shells whistle over our heads before they exploded on the island. So much for being quiet!

It took us two hours to reach shore, and there was still no opposition, even though we'd loudly announced our arrival. This further terrified me; I was sure that the enemy was just lying in wait for us. I thought of the communiqué that we had jokingly made up. We had based it on a terse English Navy communiqué: "Sighted enemy sub, sank same." Our

imaginary communiqué from the Japanese army stated: "Sighted First Special Service Force, eliminated same!" Of course, the more I thought that way, the more uneasy I became.

We pulled our boats up on the shore and apprehensively struck out for our assigned objective. We were to take, and hold, a position called Lard Hill. This "hill" was 1,000 feet above sea level, a mountain by Nova Scotia standards. Surely, I thought, the Japanese would blow us to pieces as we struggled up the slope! To my amazement and great relief, nothing happened; we suffered only the stress of always anticipating instant death. When we gained the top of Lard Hill, our mortar crew was so relieved to be alive that we almost felt we'd won a victory, George Tratt and I—the Canadian half of the crew—proudly carried out our plan to sink Canadian flags in the Aleutian soil. Then we quickly started to dig foxholes in preparation for a Japanese assault. Strange that there was still no sign of the enemy. By now, we had begun to hope for the best.

While we were digging in, O'Brien insisted on getting some logistical information. Being the efficient soldier that he was, everything had to be explicit. He hailed our company commander, Captain Gray. "What's our field of fire, sir?" was his very logical inquiry. He expected some precision—an arc of perhaps 20 degrees. But the captain was as ignorant of the situation as we were. In answer, he waved his arm through the thick fog in a rough semi-circle of 180 degrees. O'Brien returned to setting up the mortar, while shaking his head in disbelief. He kept cursing the fog, the Japanese, and the ineptitude of our officers. Smitty and I dug a foxhole together. Instead of digging straight down, we made a cavelike hole in the side of the hill. It never occurred to us that the enemy might attack from the open side of our dugout! The officers had assured us that we would be able, from this vantage point, to see the harbour of Kiska and its military installations. Strangely, they hadn't anticipated the thick fog, through which we could see about twenty-five feet. The enemy—if there were one—could be almost next to us before we'd see them.

We took turns on guard duty that night. I carried my M1 semi-automatic rifle. It was unwieldy in our cramped space, but I was used to it. Smitty, had a .45-calibre pistol. Where he acquired such a non-regulation weapon I never found out. He sat at the entrance of the cave, peering out into the foggy night. Morning came, and with it our relief—the American 87th Mountain Infantry. We could hear them approaching, then someone screamed, "You yellow bastard!" and two shots rang out. This was it! I thought, but nothing further happened. We later learned that Conchola, a Mexican-American from our unit, had been mistaken for a Japanese soldier. He'd been shot through the hand, and for some unknown reason he never rejoined the unit. That was the only combat I experienced on Kiska.

We made our way cautiously down to the shore. The beach was glutted with military supplies. Bulldozers, tanks, guns, trucks, ammunition, and boxes were strewn everywhere. Landing craft were unloading vehicles and men. It looked like utter confusion, but I figured somebody knew what they were doing. We were taken out to a ship called the *Zeilan*. I climbed up the rope ladder, and it was all I could do to reach the top. I hadn't realized that I was so tired. I was mystified, but grateful that the fearsome enemy had never materialized.

The next day, we boarded the destroyer *Kane*, and scouted other small islands in the area, but the only "prisoners" taken were two blue foxes that Herman Graf somehow captured on the island of Segula. They were beautiful, and—like so much else we'd seen here—completely foreign to us. Herman kept them, but the poor things didn't survive long when they reached the southern climate. That night we boarded another destroyer, the U.S.S. *Franklin Bell*, and sailed to Adack, where a radio broadcast made the obvious official. The Japanese, we were informed, had evacuated Kiska a few days before our arrival. Thank our lucky stars, I thought. Kiska would have been very easy to defend—even if we hadn't announced our arrival! We would have lost many men in an assault, and I might very well have been one of them. We left Adack Harbour on August 24, 1943. Our convoy had two transports, one battleship, four cruisers, and three destroyers. The thought of this great armada gave me a feeling of security. We returned, peacefully, to San Francisco.

The big news going around the ship was that one of our boys had lost one thousand dollars—a huge sum, since the average wage was sixty dollars a month! The story went that the poor fellow had gotten into a big crap game the night before we left Amchitka for Kiska. He got on a big roll, and when the game broke up he was one thousand dollars richer. He was too sensible to carry the money into battle, so he decided to bury it on Amchitka, then dig it up later and have the toot of his life. So he stuffed his winnings into a tin can for protection and buried it in the tundra, beside his tent pole. But the bigger game plan undermined his apparently sensible little scheme, which depended upon our returning to Amchitka. We didn't, and while we were gone, the service battalion took down the tents, packed our belongings, and loaded everything onto ships. That one thousand dollars is mildewing away on the cold, damp, foggy island of Amchitka! We all laughed over his wrong assumption, but I think that I'd have made the same decision. It's a loss our gambling hero will never forget! At the time, it seemed a humorous "tragedy." It still does.

We arrived in San Francisco on August 31. It was wonderful to see trees, and short green grass again and to feel the warm sun, instead of misty, damp fog. Bradley expressed our feelings exactly when he exploded with: "I hope that's the last we'll see of that godforsaken place!"

Chapter 10
O'Brien: Caught Short Fraternizing

Within two months of our "non-combat" in the Aleutians, the First Special Service Force had been moved across America and then posted overseas. That was army life, I'd come to realize: moving great distances amidst great rumour to no one knew quite where; we common soldiers usually weren't told our destination until we could see it for ourselves.

When we boarded the *Empress of Scotland*, at Norfolk, Virginia, we didn't need a general to tell us that we were crossing "the pond," or that this probably meant we'd soon be seeing action. I'd always dreamed of going to Europe, but under different circumstances. Although our ship was a luxury liner, its comforts didn't impress me much because I was preoccupied with being seasick and distracted by the constant fear of enemy attack. We were a big target, and we had no escort!

But we'd made it to Casablanca, Morocco, and now we were on the move again, feeling that we were getting closer and closer to combat. Our troop ship left Oran, Africa, November 14, 1943. Although the Mediterranean is only a "sea," it was ocean enough for me. I was seasick the first day out. Whenever I heard the anchor being pulled up, I immediately became woozy. Our trip was otherwise uneventful. We followed the African coastline, sailing within sight of Bizerte, Tunisia, then sighted the island of Sicily.

We docked in Naples on the afternoon of November 17. The city had been heavily bombed, but it was still beautiful.

Across the sparkling Bay of Naples rose the majestic cone of Vesuvius in the background. This was my first view Europe. I was thrilled, and I wished I were just a tourist, in happier times.

A few days later we arrived in the small town of Santa Maria, about twenty miles north of Naples. We were housed in a masonry building recently vacated by the Germans. They had demolished many of the rooms, but we cleaned it up and made do. "Better than a damned pup-tent," Smitty muttered, "Even if we do have to sleep on cement floors!" Smitty was right. We were out of the weather and had plenty of room for sleeping, eating, cleaning weapons, or just socializing. It was a welcome improvement.

We had just started to settle in when we were called out on parade and warned, in no uncertain terms, that "fraternizing with the Italian civilians" was strictly forbidden. We would be permitted to go so far, and no farther! We were then taken to a road outside our camp and shown our boundaries. The Italians, with their fruit, nuts, and "vino," wanted to trade with us for cigarettes and food. However, according to high command, there was an invisible line running right down the centre of that road. The Italians could not cross that line and mix with the military, and we couldn't cross it to "fraternize" with them.

We obeyed these rules strictly—and simplistically. The line, though invisible, was never crossed intentionally, but even though no one stepped across the imaginary line a brisk trade instantly sprung up between us. Apples, tangerines, nuts, and wine were passed across the line, in exchange for cigarettes and rations. We bought things from them, using "occupation money,"—the small, crisp, new paper bills printed by the allies for use in occupied countries. It looked fake to us, but was readily accepted as currency by the local people.

Jim O'Brien was the keenest bargainer in my mortar crew, but his interest was in Italian wine, not food. Being hard-nosed and businesslike, he wasn't satisfied with just any wine; he wanted the best they had to offer, and the only way to make sure that he got it was to sample their wares. That was a big mistake!

O'Brien had always maintained that he could eat and drink anything, and he'd always backed up his claim. I'd often heard Tratt observe, after O'Brien had eaten enough for six men: "That O.B.'s got an iron stomach!" But this mixture of wine samples proved to be our hero's downfall. (O'Brien's behaviour on this occasion and his extreme comeuppance, reminded me of my old pal Woodard, back in the artillery unit.)

The poor man staggered in, after a long round of "wine-tasting." Dead drunk, he struggled out of his boots, then he crawled into his sleeping bag, fully clothed. He still had the presence of mind to pull the zipper all the way up—another big mistake!

We were lucky enough to have down-filled sleeping bags—called "fart sacks" by some of the cruder fellows. They were wonderfully cosy, and much warmer than blankets, but they had one aggravating flaw—the zipper would get stuck And it often took a lot of struggling and cursing before you could free yourself—even when you had all your wits about you.

It wasn't long after Tratt, Smitty, and I had settled down for the night that the predictable happened. We were rudely awakened by poor O'Brien, pleading for help. His iron stomach had rusted out, and his bowels had gotten the better of him. There's no good time to have the "runs" (or the "galloping trots," as we sometimes called this condition), but there are especially bad times—and for O'Brien, this was a bad time. The zipper of his sleeping bag was stuck. He was trapped! The tugging, the pulling, the cursing was to no avail. O'Brien pleaded with us to help him, but although we loved him dearly, and respected him, there are limits to friendship. Instead of rushing to his aid, we beat a hasty retreat to the other end of the barracks.

Poor O'Brien continued struggling, and cursing his buddies who had deserted him in his hour of need. We would have rushed through enemy fire to help our comrade, but the odour coming from his sleeping bag was more than we could endure. Finally the zipper gave way, and O'Brien rushed out. Eventually he returned, white as a sheet, muttering how he would get his revenge on us. We were snickering in the corner, but we made damn sure that he didn't hear us!

He spent the rest of the night and all the next day washing his clothes and sleeping bag. He washed, and washed again, using soap and any kind of disinfectant he could lay his hands on. He was thorough, as only O'Brien could be. He kept mumbling that the use of sleeping bags was a real foul-up. The army should return to using blankets! At last he was confident that the odour had been expunged, so he hung his clothes and sleeping bag outside to dry.

We never brought up the episode in O'Brien's presence. I noticed, though, that he learned two lessons from his misfortune. I never again saw him drink even a drop of Italian wine, and he never, ever, zipped up his sleeping bag when he retired for the night.

Chapter 11

Our Baptism of Fire

Our unit, the First Special Service Force, saw its first action in December of 1943. Although we were highly trained, we had never been in combat; neither had our officers.

The American 5th Army's advance into Italy was being slowed down because the Germans held many strategic mountaintops north of Naples. Because of our mountain-climbing skills, we were ordered to take one of these peaks—Monte La Difensa, elevation 3,500 feet. It was strategically important, because it had a commanding view of the surrounding countryside, including the main highway. The enemy could rain down artillery fire on any troops moving along this road. Other major attacks on this bastion had failed, but the strategists thought that our unit, being fresh and well trained, could take the position.

The plan called for a surprise attack, under cover of darkness, and I remember the night well. It was cold, raining, and pitch black when our regiment—about five hundred men—started trudging up the mountain's only path. We wore rain capes, and our weapons included rifles, tommy guns, machine guns, mortars, and bazookas. It was so dark that each man held onto the bayonet scabbard of the man in front of him to keep contact. I later learned that this was a mistake only "green" soldiers would make. By keeping so close our casualties would be much higher if a shell landed among us. I learned, too, that experience is a cruel teacher.

As we slogged along, slipping and sliding on the wet, muddy path, someone behind began muttering. I recognized the voice of Byrom, a big tough guy from Texas. He was muttering this same thing over and over, and when I finally made out what he was saying, it sent shivers up and down my spine, because it seemed so much out of character. "I was meant to be a lover, not a soldier ... I was meant to a lover, not a soldier ... I was meant. ..." No matter how often the officers whispered: "Shhh ... shhh," Byrom kept repeating his mournful dirge. He sounded terrified but resigned, and my thoughts flashed back to my childhood, when my mother and father would talk of "forerunners" and premonitions. Someone would say, "I'm not going to last through the night," and they'd be dead by dawn. A knock on the door or tap on the window without anyone being there meant that there would be a death in the family. How scared I'd become when they talked about these unnatural events.

Suddenly there was a great flash of light and a tremendous explosion. I looked in horror as bodies, and parts of bodies, were flung skyward. I later learned that Byrom had been blasted off the side of the mountain. The artillery shells kept raining down on us, and the exploded shells left a strange smell that I couldn't identify, but that I'd recognize even today.

Between the shell bursts I could hear the screams and moans of my wounded and dying comrades who had been blown down the side of the mountain. The pitiful cries floated up to us as we kept struggling along the slippery path. My mind raced far ahead of my slipping feet. What kind of a hell was this? No enemy in sight, but they were slaughtering us! How precious the dull, humdrum life of Truro suddenly seemed to me.

The yelling and groaning became more discernible. Most of the victims screamed one of two phrases as they fought with every fibre of their being to stay alive. "Oh, Jesus! Oh Jesus!" I heard; but more often "Oh, Jesus Christ! Oh, Jesus Christ! Oh, Jesus Christ!" But the saddest utterance came from one poor soldier who was pouring out his heart along with his heart's blood. "Mama! Mama! Mama!" he pleaded, crying out for the person dearest to him in the world.

The officers soon realized that we were losing too many men, and the order came down the line to "dig in." I more than welcomed the chance to hide from this inferno! It was too dark to see anything, and in my fright I dove headfirst off the path into the bank of the mountain. I felt a terrific impact on my head, and everything went black! When I regained consciousness I realized that I had gone head-to-head with a giant boulder!

I heard the scrape of shovels and immediately loosened my entrenching tool from my belt and started digging in. I dug feverishly, thinking that if a boulder got in my way, I'd plough right through it! I was still digging when the order came: "Form up on the path; we're pulling back!" We all lined up on the path and filed back down the mountain. Our training and discipline really paid off at this point. Although there were shells bursting all around us and we had never experienced this before, there was no panic, no stampede; just cool action and instinctive obeying of orders.

At the base of the mountain, we sank exhausted under the trees. I was very, very tired, but my nerves wouldn't let me sleep. My clothes were soaked, I was very cold, and my neck ached from my head-on collision with the mountainside. Well, I figured, if I couldn't sleep, I'd eat. (Eating was always a passion with me, and my capacity was a joke in the unit.) I took a package of "K" rations from my backpack and started to open it. I noticed my hands were shaking. My introduction to warfare had rattled me more than I cared to admit. I looked over at my buddy, O'Brien. He, too, was trying to open his ration box, and his hands shook as much as my own. O'Brien grinned sheepishly and said, "It's so damned cold here isn't it?" I quickly agreed, but we both knew that the cold had little to do with the way we were shaking.

O'Brien, Tratt, Smitty, and I talked until daylight. How many of our friends had been hit? How many wounded? How many killed? We knew we'd lost a good many buddies, but we had no idea how numerous the casualties really were. We later learned that our regiment had lost nearly forty percent of its strength the first night in the combat area—and we hadn't even seen the enemy yet! Our first action had made a tremendous impression on all of us. No more would we think of war as being chivalrous, or romantic. "War is hell" would never again sound like a cliché! Our homes and loved ones now seemed very remote—and very precious.

At the first light of dawn came a request for volunteers for the unenviable job of returning up the trail to bring back the dead and wounded. Because I was quite big and strong, I felt that I should go. We wore Red Cross bands on our arms to show the enemy that we were on a mission of mercy. The narrow, steep, slippery path made carrying stretchers a difficult task, but the physical strain seemed a minor discomfort when we looked at the dead and wounded.

We carried down corpses and men who wished they were dead. We carried down men who were deliriously happy to still be alive, even though some were missing arms, legs, or both; some were blinded, and others had horrible internal wounds.

Handling these casualties had a profound effect on me. These were men—friends, comrades—who, only a few short hours before, had been perfect specimens of manhood. They were buddies with whom we'd shared a year and a half of intensive training. A few hours before, they had joked and laughed and shared their dreams and future plans with us. Now they would never be the same—and neither would we.

Next came the gruesome task of burying the dead. We dug individual rectangular holes and lowered the bodies in. It was then that I learned why we each carried two dog-tags. One of them was buried with the body for future identification; the other was sent home with his other personal belongings, to his next of kin.

Night was coming on by the time we finished our sad task. We thought we'd finally have some rest, but we were shocked into activity when our company commander yelled his order: "Saddle up! We're going back up again!" We adjusted our backpacks, checked our weapons, and formed up at the base of the mountain. "We're taking a different approach tonight," the officer said. "We're going up the mountain from the other side." (This was our introduction to another characteristic of war. Orders would often come, when least expected, from we knew not where, to do what seemed impossible. Our job was to obey them, instantly and without question.)

It was dark when we started out, but the rain had stopped, which was something to be thankful for. O'Brien, Smitty, Tratt, and I stayed as close together as we could. About three in the morning, after a quiet ascent, we reached a flat area about two-thirds of the way up the mountain. It looked like a good place to take a much-needed rest. Luckily for us, the officers agreed. We had just removed our packs and started getting comfortable when we heard the ominous whine of artillery shells, which began bursting close by. Our thoughts went back to the previous night's disaster, and this made us very edgy—to say the least.

As the shell-bursts came closer and closer, and we became more and more frightened. Tratt, O'Brien, and Smitty erupted, spontaneously, into argument. It was a bizarre, stupid, pathetic, useless, humorous argument, which, considering the circumstances, I'll never forget. Tratt was of the firm conviction that the shells that were landing so close were from German artillery. O'Brien knew, he claimed, that the whine was definitely that of American shells coming in. Smitty felt certain that it was the English artillery, because they were on our right flank, and the firing seemed to come from that direction. I made no argument as to whose shells they were; I just buried my face in good old Mother Earth, and sought any shelter I could find! Who cared whether the shells were British or American, instead of German?

I soon learned that the terrible strain of waiting out a heavy bombardment often provoked outlandish behaviours. Few people can remain calm while helplessly awaiting annihilation!

This time, we were lucky! Eventually the artillery fire petered out and all was still again. An hour-and-a-half had passed since we had stopped to rest. The respite came to an abrupt end when we heard a terrific firefight break out at the peak of the mountain. "My God!" yelled Tratt, "Our Second regiment must have reached the top!" (This was later confirmed.) We could hear rifle fire, machine-gun fire, and mortar fire. "We'd better get the hell up there!" one of our officers shouted. We saddled up again, with our packboards and our weapons. I carried the base-plate of our mortar, along with my rifle and ammunition. I also had my rations and water bottle. The next leg of our climb was much more difficult. The mountain became steeper, and in some places it was necessary to use ropes to get up the near-perpendicular outcroppings. Gradually the firing died out, and we could only hope that our second regiment had taken its objective.

The result of the battle became apparent when, just an hour after sunrise, we heard some activity on the trail above us. Two men from our unit appeared on the flat part of the trail, followed by a large number of unarmed Germans. More of our men brought up the rear of the column. They looked weary, but also relieved that the battle was over and that they had successfully completed their first mission.

Now we got our first close-up look at the enemy. I was shocked that they were so clean! Their uniforms were neat, and they looked as though they were heading for the parade square. Our men, on the other hand, looked muddy, dirty, and unkempt. We looked more like the losers than the winners! It fascinated me that our enemies looked just like us. I don't know what I expected: maybe big, tough, gangster-type hoods—men definitely vile and despicable-looking. But they were just clean cut, very young, and very ordinary-looking men.

This was my first good look at their uniforms—with the distinctive helmets and high black boots. What really caught my attention, and then deeply disturbed me, was their belts. The buckle had an eagle on it, and the inscription "Gott Mit Uns." "God is with us." Such absolute assurance shocked me. *I* was absolutely certain that *we* were in the right. Surely God was on *our* side! How could mortal enemies both be certain that their cause had the blessing of the Almighty! This disturbed me very much, and I pondered on it often throughout the war—and after it.

After more rope-climbing, we reached the almost flat summit and relieved the second regiment. We congratulated them on their success, and they headed down the mountain, leaving us in charge of the position, including the dead and the wounded—both friend and enemy. We settled in, making ourselves as comfortable as possible. I picked a place behind a huge boulder where I could sit and look over the valley. I thought that I was looking towards friendly lines; how wrong I was! As I was relaxing that night, covered with a blanket and rain cape, I was shaken into full consciousness by an eerie and frightening noise that I'd never heard before. It sounded like continuous groaning, interspersed with tremendous explosions.

I suddenly felt very vulnerable alone in the dark, and I became very alarmed! I felt that the guns flashing in the valley were aimed directly at me—and me alone. Within split seconds I'd grabbed my rain cape, blanket, backpack, helmet, and rifle, and beat a hasty retreat around to the other side of the protective boulder! There I lay, face-down, until the shelling ended. I only looked up when I heard shouts from my buddies around me, and found out that no one had been hit. Everyone, though, had been shaken by this scary-sounding weapon that was new to us all. I later learned that this was the notorious German seven-barrelled rocket launcher. They called it "Neblewerfer"; we called it "moaning Minnie," or "screaming meemie," which seemed to fit its frightening sound and the effect it had on us. I think we stayed on top of Monte La Difensa, in the rain and cold, for five days and nights. We had set up defensive positions, in preparation for a counterattack— which never came, thank goodness!

One of those days, while I was sitting and gazing over the valley, I saw one of our Piper Cub planes float lazily by. It was nearly at eye level with me because I was so high on the mountain peak. It looked perfectly peaceful, as it gently dipped from left to right, and swooped around like a giant bird. Piper Cubs were used as observation planes. They were very slow, but also very manoeuvrable, so they made wonderful spotters to direct artillery and observe enemy movement. They must have been a pesky aggravation to the Germans. I was jarred out of my daydreaming when two silver-coloured Messerschmitts zoomed out of nowhere and pounced on our little Piper Cub! I heard the "rat-tat-tat" of machine guns, and the spotter plane plummeted to the ground. The two German planes disappeared as quickly as they had appeared. I turned my attention anxiously to the Piper Cub. To my relief, I saw something separate from the cockpit, and then a beautiful white parachute blossomed out. The pilot floated slowly down into the valley. I watched helplessly as he landed in a field and enemy troops came out from a fringe of woods to take him prisoner. I let out a sigh of relief. At least he was alive!

The Third Regiment of our unit had the arduous task of bringing supplies up the mountain. They sweated, strained, fell, picked themselves up again, and kept doggedly on until they reached the top: they acted, in fact, like pack animals. The difference was that they were a little more stubborn and determined than the animals would have been. They carried cans of water, ammunition, mortar shells, food, first-aid supplies, and many other necessities. Laden down with these tremendous loads, they slipped and slid on the narrow muddy path. On the steeper grades they had to use scaling ropes! Going down, they had to carry the dead and wounded. They made trip after trip, although they were exhausted. We were completely dependent on the lifeline provided by our comrades: without these precious supplies we couldn't have held the mountaintop.

We never appreciated them so much, however, as on the day they became our Santa Clauses! We were cold, wet, and miserable until we saw that, strapped onto packboards which had just arrived were—wonder of wonders—cases of whisky! Morale skyrocketed! The solemn, uncomfortable faces of a few minutes before were now smiling, joking, and laughing.

Being a teetotaler, I suddenly became one of the most popular guys on the hill. Many, many newfound friends were willing to take my ration of liquor off my hands, but I had other plans. My share went to Tratt, Smitty, and O'Brien—except for some that I gave to Bob Maco, a friend in distress. I could hear Bob groaning, and when I went to have a look, he was curled up in his makeshift foxhole holding his stomach. "My guts are on fire!" he moaned. I had a brainstorm and assured him that I knew the cure for his problem. I hurried off and returned with a canteen mug, half filled with whisky! Bob savoured each drop, and his immediate improvement was remarkable! He told me later that I had saved his life. Bob's over seventy now and in good health. To this day he says to me, "You know, Peppard, ever since you gave me that whisky, my stomach has never bothered me since!"

Strangely, after my whisky ration was gone my newfound

friends vanished too! The liquor had served its purpose, though. The mood on the summit of Monte La Difensa improved, and morale remained very high. Two days later we were relieved by part of the American 36th Division.

As we wound our way down the mountain, I got separated from the rest of my platoon. I'd dropped my rain cape, and doubled back to get it. When I turned around again, there was no one in sight. Suddenly, artillery shells began bursting behind me, so I speeded it up down the only path. The explosion was too far back to be dangerous to me, but the next one was closer. The shells seemed to have eyes of their own. They kept following me right down the path. My God, I thought: the Germans must have zeroed in on this path before they retreated! It was then I took off in earnest. As the shells came closer and closer, the faster and faster I ran, closely followed by earth-shattering explosions and showers of rocks. I was running so fast, I'm certain Jesse Owens would have gazed at me in envy! More than once I was airborne—both feet off the ground and still pumping! As I reached level ground, I saw my salvation—a large outcropping of rock. If I could get behind that, I would be safe. With a last burst of energy I hurled myself behind the shelter.

As I sank down, exhausted, behind this welcome shelter, I realized that I was not alone. There stood four of my buddies, relaxing around a "Dixie" of steaming coffee (A Dixie was what we called the hugh containers that held gallons of coffee, or other liquid.) and an enormous box of doughnuts! I couldn't believe my eyes. Beside them stood Getty Page, his big Red Cross band on his arm, larger than life—as were all the members of that organization, who walked, routinely, into the inferno to bring a little comfort and reason into this sordid affair. I'll never forget him, his organization, or the feeling of warmth and contentment I felt on that rainy day. Miracles do happen—at the strangest times, and in the strangest places!

Thus ended my first week of war. I had already seen and endured horrors that I'd rather have done without—and this was just the beginning! But I was encouraged by a small voice deep within me, saying over and over again, "You're going to survive this war. You're going to survive this war." And I believed that voice.

Chapter 12

There's No Tomorrow

As I got older and bolder, the stories of the supernatural I'd heard as a child seemed little more than fairy tales. No longer did I hang back when a tap came at the door. I would rush to answer it, confident that there would be someone there—and there always was. So I trod fearlessly into the future, knowing that only the gullible swallowed such superstitions. But then—in the army—experience shook my "rational" conviction. When Sergeant Byrom began his mournful dirge as we climbed Monte La Difensa he was, I am certain, having a vision of his death—which was realized only moments later.

A few nights later, I witnessed even more convincing evidence that people have true premonitions. Just before we moved out, I overheard Staff-Sergeant Roderick having a heart-to-heart talk with his friend, George Wright. "George," he said sorrowfully, "I won't be coming back from this one. I'm going to be killed tonight." "That's foolish!" George answered. "Nobody knows that! No one can see into the future!" "I can," was the reply. "I know for certain I'll die tonight." "Well, for God's sake, beg off!" shouted George. "Say you're sick, or hurt, or something like that!" "No, no, I just couldn't do that," Roderick said. "They'd say I was yellow."

Our objective was only 1,500 yards from our starting position, but in the mountains you cannot travel in a straight line, as on a map. Three miles—and many peaks and gullies—later, we were still trudging along with no sign of our goal. Suddenly two machine guns opened up on us. We could see the tracer bullets coming towards us. Of course, we could only see the tracers, but between two tracers there were usually ten regular bullets.

Just as we hit the ground I heard a groan about twenty yards away. I knew it was Roderick, because he had been next to me in the single file. I wormed my way over to him. It was so dark that I couldn't see his face, but as I turned him over, my hands became wet and sticky with blood.

I asked him if he was all right, but he didn't answer, so I figured he was unconscious. I knew he was alive, because I could hear him breathing. I felt he needed first aid immediately, so I started yelling for a medic. I searched through my pack for something warm to wrap round him, but all I could find was an extra pair of pants. I covered him as best I could. (Incidentally, my pants had my name stamped on them, and someone found them later, and thought I had been killed.)

Finally a medic got to us. He examined Roderick and then muttered: "This guy's dead." "He can't be!" I yelled. "He's still breathing!" "No, he's dead." said the medic, with a note of finality. "Besides his chest wound, he has a bullet hole right through his head!" "But he was breathing!" I protested. "That's natural," said the medic, "but it's not breathing, it's just air escaping from his lungs."

We left Roderick lying there, and continued on to our objective. As I stumbled along, I recalled the events of the past few days. How could I doubt that people sometimes peer into the future and predict what will happen to them in the next few hours? I could never deny that two of my friends *knew* that they were going to die within hours, and that their premonitions came true.

Chapter 13

Christmas Day, 1943

"What mountain is this?" growled Tiny Beacon, as the company trudged upward along the narrow path. "I heard an officer call it Hill 720," said Bradley. "What's 720 mean?" I asked. "Must be the height," said Tiny. I craned my neck to try to see the top, but the rain blocked out my view. "It sure looks higher than 720 feet!" "That's metres," Tiny explained. "That would make it over 2,200 feet!" said Bradley. "Where do these officers get off calling this a hill?" "Well at least it's not quite as high or steep as Monte La Difensa!" I panted. We were laden down—as usual—with weapons, ammunition, and rations. With each step, the straps of the rucksack cut deeper into my shoulders.

I thought back to the parade we'd had at Santa Maria nearly two weeks before—just after our baptism of fire. General Mark Clark, commander of The American Fifth Army, had talked to us. He'd praised us highly for securing our difficult objective. Most of us had thought that his next words would be: "I'm going to give you all a four-week leave to Naples!" Instead he'd shattered our dreams—and our naivety—with: "You'll have bigger and better hills to climb!"

So here we were, trudging up Hill 720, in the cold, cold rain, on December 23, 1943. The general had decided to give us a break on the size, I figured.

The order filtered down the column: "Take ten." We shuffled off the path, removed our packs, and tried to get comfortable.

As we were resting, two men appeared on the path, heading for the summit. The one in front carried a crude walking stick, and although straight and slim, he looked older than the rest of us. It was hard to see his face under his parka, but I'd have guessed his age to be nearly forty. "My God!" Tratt said, "I didn't think we had any old men in this outfit!" "That's not just any old man!" snorted Bradley, with a note of admiration in his voice. "That's the Old Man himself!" "What Old Man?" some of us asked. "The Old Man! The Old Man! The commander of the First Special Service Force. That's Colonel Frederick himself!" "What the hell's he doin' way up here?" asked Slim in disbelief. "You know his reputation," said Bradley. "He believes in leading his men, not pushing them." "Yeah! But he could get hurt leadin' that way!" Slim interjected. "Tell him, don't tell me. He's already been wounded three times," said Bradley proudly. (Colonel Frederick went on to receive *seven* wounds while leading our unit.)

As we lay on the sodden ground wet, and with teeth chattering, I turned to Slim Martell and confided in him. "I wonder what it's like to be dead?" I asked, a little embarrassed. "Whata ya mean?" Slim snarled. "Well, when I dove into a rock on La Difensa, I was knocked out for awhile. Everything went black. I didn't know a thing; I didn't feel a thing, until I came to." "Well, what about it? That's the way death will be!" Slim said emphatically. "I don't see it that way," I said, a little self-consciously. "I believe our souls go to some sort of place—like heaven, or another dimension. Then we'll see friends and relatives who've died before us." "That's a lot of bullshit we've been fed since we were kids! When you're dead, you're dead. You won't know nothin', you won't feel nothin', you won't see nothin'. In fact that's just what you'll be—nothin'!" "Well, I believe there's something after death. I believe the Almighty wouldn't let things end in death. We'll exist in another place." "The Almighty!" snorted Slim. "There ain't no such thing! It's just another fairy tale. Do you think

"The Old Man" leads the way. Colonel Frederick, C. O. of the force, in the Italian mountains, 1943. He not only led his men into their most dangerous battles, he usually got to their destination ahead of them.

if there was some good, almighty being, he'd let this bloody war go on! Thousands are being killed and murdered!" I was on the defensive then. "You can't blame God for wars. Wars are man-made!" "Well, that may be so, but I still think when you're dead, you're dead! After that there's nothin'! If you believe differently, you're in for a big surprise when your time comes." This seemed a contradiction in terms, because if everything was black, and you knew nothing, how could you be surprised? Our deep philosophical discussion was interrupted by Lieutenant Gray. "You two guys go with this artillery officer, and make sure he doesn't get hit!"

We accompanied the forward observation officer until he reached a vantage point where we could see German soldiers below us on a smaller hill. There were about forty of them. They were unaware of us, because they were concentrating on defending their hill. They were firing machine guns and rifles at soldiers we couldn't see. They were out of range of Slim's rifle, and my tommy gun might as well have been a peashooter at that distance. The artillery officer, on the other hand, was in his glory—this was what the war was all about, for him.

He set up his radio equipment, and after studying his map he radioed back a coordinate. "Fire one!" he ordered. We heard a shell scream over our heads and saw it explode short of the target. "Raise three hundred!" he ordered. The next shell overshot the Germans, who had instinctively crouched down, as though that might protect them. That was exactly what I did under artillery fire. "Lower one hundred!" shouted the officer, a look of satisfaction on his face. This shell landed right in among the enemy, who scrambled for shelter. "Fire for effect!" he shouted triumphantly. Then the enemy hill became a raging inferno as a battery miles behind us poured shell upon shell into it. Finally the officer radioed back: "Cease fire."

I couldn't help but feel sorry for the soldiers exposed to such a battering. I could make out about eight bodies sprawled out down there. Some others may have been wounded, but they had concealed themselves in foxholes and dugouts. "Twenty dead!" shouted the officer into his radio set. Then he turned to us and said: "You got to exaggerate to keep those boys happy back there."

Then and there, I became suspicious of all army communiqués and all newscasts pertaining to the war and to casualties. Lieutenant Gray ordered Slim and me to rejoin our platoons, as the artillery officer packed up his gear.

Christmas Eve saw us clearing the Germans off the hilltop, but only at tragic expense. A mortar shell landed close to my three best buddies, and just like that Smitty, my dearest friend and confidante was dead. His death was a terrible blow to me, but there was little time for grieving. Tratt and O'Brien, who were with Smitty, were wounded by the same shell.

*George Smith (Smitty), my best buddy ever since training, was
killed in action on Christmas Eve, 1943.*

We dug in after that to secure our positions, each man to his own foxhole. Christmas Day 1943 dawned rainy and cold. I thought about home. I thought about the hot, cosy wood stove, with a couple of chickens roasting in the oven. "Pep! Pep!" I heard Tiny Beacon call from the next foxhole. I poked my head out cautiously. Mortar shells were landing around us occasionally. "What ya got to eat?" "I'll see," I yelled to him. I rifled through my boxes of K rations. "I got a couple of cans of meat, I think they're Spam!" "I've got a couple of cans of cheese," yelled Tiny, "but I like Spam better. How about a trade?" We agreed and threw each other a can.

I sat up as much as I could without exposing my head, and I opened my can of cheese. It looked very good to me. I took one of my four dry crackers and scooped some cheese out with it. I washed it down with some stale water from my water bottle. I was determined to enjoy my meal, even in a wet foxhole on top of a rainswept mountain amidst sporadic mortar fire. "Pep! Pep!" Tiny called again. "Yeah?" I peeped over the rim of my foxhole and saw Tiny's big helmet and dirty face. A smile crinkled his mud-stained face, as he shouted above the explosions: "Merry Christmas, Pep!"

Chapter 14
Axis Sally

We were in a makeshift rest area, between combat missions in the mountains. Life seemed good, which just proves how relative things are. We slept in two-man pup tents that were only about three feet high at their peak. Their purpose was just to cover the two bodies as we slept. We had hot food, because a field kitchen had been set up. There was no shelling, and as far as I was concerned, there was no war. It was during such a respite that I was given the dubious benefit of a promotion. I was made a staff sergeant, with no choice and with the attendant responsibilities. The reason for my being bumped up was not encouraging; we were suffering such heavy losses that somebody had to do it.

I lounged around, dry, warm, and contented. I wrote letters home to Mum and Greta. The relaxation, and the time of year (it was just after Christmas) made me homesick. I wondered whether Greta would meet someone and get married. That worried me. Then I thought I was being very foolish, because our three glorious dates during my eleven days at home hardly established a lasting relationship. Still, in my heart of hearts, I often dreamed of Greta. I dreamed of us getting married, of starting a family, of raising that family, and of growing old together. I was jarred out of my daydreaming by Jim O'Brien. "Let's take a walk through camp, Pep."

We passed row upon row of pup tents and joked with some of the guys we knew. One guy hollered: "My God, O'Brien, are you still alive?" A bunch of guys were gathered around the large tent that was used for headquarters. We heard a radio playing, so we joined them just as a beautiful, melodious female voice, speaking in English, came over the airwaves. We looked expectantly at some of the guys. They filled us in: "It's Axis Sally, that German propaganda broad, broadcasting from Rome," they told us. "She's reading a list of the prisoners of war." It was a long list! Sally gave the names and serial numbers of Allied soldiers who had been captured, then she spoke to us. She talked, it seemed, to each of us in a confidential manner that reminded me of my grade six teacher, Miss Feetham—scolding, but friendly. I can't remember exactly what she said, but his was this gist of it: Why are you Americans and Canadians fighting thousands of miles from your homes? This is not your war! This is England's war. Don't sacrifice your lives for the English; they're just using you as cannon fodder! Remember, there's a loving family waiting for you at home! Then Sally's voice faded out and a haunting melody started to play. Another female voice, as beautiful as Axis Sally's, started singing.

> Mid pleasures and palaces though I may roam,
> Be it ever so humble, there's no place like home.

As the song continued, my mind flashed back to Truro. I thought of our house, on Alice Street, surrounded by a white picket fence. I pictured my mother, my father, my five sisters, and three brothers. That was the home this wonderful song was all about.

When the broadcast ended, there was a lot of loud laughing and crude jokes about Axis Sally, and the singer. Vulgarity was another way we hid our true feelings from each other throughout the war. I'm certain that as we bedded down in our tents that night many a tear fell from a homesick eye.

I tossed and turned, my mind was drifting between home and that nostalgic song.

Home, home sweet sweet home
There's no place like home
There's no place like home!

I did eventually fall asleep, but before I did, I remember cursing with a vengeance: "Damn that Axis Sally!"

Chapter 15
Take Me Back to the Front!

George Bradley had just rejoined our unit in the mountains, after being in the army hospital. He had not been wounded in action but had suffered an affliction that caused fifty percent of our casualties—trench feet. Our medical officer, Major Neseman, preferred the more modern and less alarming name "athlete's foot." No matter what he called it, the condition was nonetheless painful; it was caused by the feet being continually wet and cold, and by lack of circulation. Huge cracks would open between the toes, causing painful swelling and bleeding.

Bradley came back with a head full of stories about his hospital experiences; and when you're in the field, such diversions are welcome. He began by torturing us with descriptions of the food, and the beautiful nurses who'd treated him like a hero. The beds were soft, he claimed, with spotless white sheets. "I'd forgotten what it was like to sleep in a bed like that." So had we all!

"But there's always some damn thing to spoil it," he said disgustedly. "Those bloody eggheads took all the joy out of my stay in the hospital!" "Eggheads?" we asked. "Yes, eggheads; they're the psychiatrists who give you all those tests to see if you're cracking up under the strain of combat! They don't say you're crazy. They call it 'battle fatigue'!" We'd been hearing talk recently about this new thing—battle fatigue—but Bradley was the only person we knew who'd been tested for it. Naturally, we were curious. "What kind of tests?" we asked. "Well," said Bradley, warming up to his story, "They gave me a written exam, and then one of the doctors discussed my answers with me." "Was the exam hard?" "Not hard, but tricky. But they didn't fool me. I remembered that the first and fifth questions were exactly alike, but worded differently, to throw you off." "So you did OK?" "I thought so, until the psychiatrist took me into his office and started to question me. He stared at me a long time and then told me that he was very disturbed with my answer to question twenty-six. I didn't know what he meant, but he looked really upset. When I didn't say anything, he told me that it was the most important question of the test. 'I'll refresh your memory. Question twenty-six asked: If a genie appeared out of a bottle and said it would grant you only one wish, what would your wish be? Do you remember the answer you gave?' 'Sure,' I told him. 'I wrote that I wish the war would end right away.' As soon as I said that, his eyes bugged out, and he looked at me as if he couldn't believe his ears, I began to wonder about his sanity. 'Why would you say a thing like that, Bradley?' and he was really agitated. 'Because that's the way I feel!' I told him. I wish this war was over!' "

We all knew exactly what Bradley meant. We'd have answered exactly the same thing. But according to our buddy, that was a "wrong" answer, and the doctor took it as evidence of Bradley's being a bad soldier. "When I told him how terrible war was, he just told me that I'd volunteered, and that I had a defeatist attitude. He told me that I should be proud to serve my country. Well that made *me* mad, and I said to him, 'That's easy for you to say! You're here.' 'Enough of your snivelling excuses!' he said to me. 'Your job is to go back to the front, and do your duty like a man! We all have our trials and tribulations and hardships to bear!' So that was that. On my way out, a ward boy was taking this long suffering, overworked doctor his doughnuts and fresh coffee. And he thought *I* was crazy! Promise me, guys, if I'm ever wounded again, patch me up as best you can, but don't send me back to army hospital!"

Chapter 16

A Reason to Laugh

After fighting in the mountains, we returned to Santa Maria for a rest. It was great pleasure and relief to be out of combat conditions. We had a roof covering us, hot food, and, best of all, nobody was trying to kill us! We slept in sleeping bags on a cement floor, but we were so happy and relaxed that, just before we went to sleep, someone gave a heartfelt yell: "Wake me up when the war's over!" Our sentiments exactly, and we all laughed in appreciation.

This respite was short-lived, however. A few days later, we were rushed by boat to the Anzio Beachhead. On the evening of February 2, 1944, we took up position on the line. Our regiment was on the right flank, bordering the Tyrennian Sea. Our line was along the banks of the Mussolini Canal, which drained the Pontine Marshes.

We were told that the entire area had been underwater until Mussolini came to power. Under his government's supervision, the marshes were drained into canals that carried the water out to sea, and neat little masonry farmhouses were built on the reclaimed land. In exchange for land and houses, the farmers returned part of their crops to the government.

The beachhead had been secured a couple of weeks before. The Allied aim was to split the German forces, and thereby hasten the fall of Rome. But the Allies were stymied by three things—a shortage of men, the unexpectedly strong German opposition, and the difficulty of the terrain. The beachhead was on flat land, and the surrounding hills were held by the enemy. Thus we were under constant observation and frequent artillery fire. We remained stuck on the Anzio Beachhead for four interminable months, before we were able to break out.

The little village of Borgo Sabatino was directly in front of us and became part of our line of defence. The officer in charge of this village was Captain Gus Heilman, from Pennsylvania, so we soon renamed the village "Gusville." The main house in this village became a gathering place for us, when we weren't on the lines and when the house wasn't being shelled. Many a chicken, egg, or pig brought back from evening patrols, was cooked in that little farmhouse.

Gus Heilman's two righthand men were Lieutenant Krasevac, from Nevada, and Sergeant Spud Wright, from Alberta. Spud was a good friend of mine. The exploits of these two in No-Man's-Land were daring and astoundingly successful. One night they set a trap that captured 35 Germans who were preparing an attack on Gusville. Later, two other groups wandered into the trap, and they too were taken prisoner. The final tally came to 111 captured! The next day, the prisoners were marched down the road to the rear. To see so many of the enemy unarmed and looking so dejected really boosted my morale. I thought the war was over! Of course it soon dawned on me that 111 is a drop in the bucket when you considered the millions of soldiers in the German Army.

When I thought of Gus Heilman, Spud Wright, and Krasevac, it was one of the few times I felt sympathy for the enemy. I certainly wouldn't want to be facing those three guys! Spud went on the receive the Distinguished Service Cross, the second-highest award given in the American army. He also received the Military Medal from the Canadian government.

Spud paid a great price, however, in earning his medals. While leading a platoon in southern France, he captured some enemy troops, but an officer and two other men escaped and fled down a deep ditch. Spud took off after them alone, and the German officer suddenly turned, whipped out his Luger and shot Spud just above his eye. Spud was in hospital for quite some time. Gradually, his memory came back. He returned to the unit and continued his daring exploits.

Fifty yards from headquarters at Gusville, two roads converged. At this junction a .50-calibre machine gun emplacement was dug in. John Landriault and a buddy named Gilbert (both from Ontario) were manning the position. John was a friend of mine. One morning at dawn, John got the surprise of his life. He looked out of his dugout into the eyes of two German soldiers. They seemed to be lost, and each was pushing a bicycle. Apparently, they had just returned from leave, and must have taken a wrong turn. They were looking with great surprise at the strange weapon in the dugout.

When John popped his head up, they realized he was definitely *not* a German soldier, and they were galvanized into action. They both sprang onto their bikes to beat a hasty retreat, but John, and his buddy had other ideas. They leaped out, grabbed the parcel carrier of one of the bicycles, and pulled back with all their strength. The German stood straight up on his pedals, giving it everything he had. Despite his best efforts, however, the bicycle came to a sliding stop, and he and his bicycle were taken prisoner. Meanwhile, the other soldier was making a speedy getaway. John jumped down into the gun pit and opened fire with the machine gun, but the German soldier made good his escape. He was going so fast, John told us later, that even a bullet couldn't catch him.

Although our unit had only two thousand fighting men, and we were spread thinly along a line that should have been occupied by a division, our commanding officer, Colonel Frederick, felt that our force should continue to show an offensive attitude. I suppose he thought that this would be better for morale and might also confuse the enemy about our numbers. With this in mind, we were often in action at night—

German prisoners helping carry out the wounded, Italy, January 1944.

on patrol, fighting patrol, or manning "listening posts," far in advance of our lines. The soldiers at these listening posts were well armed, and they had telephones to keep in communication with our lines.

A comical incident happened to a buddy of mine named Harry. Harry and Jerome were manning a listening-post one night, about a mile ahead of our lines. Every hour Harry would report back to our lines; usually he'd say: "Charlie?

*The Special Service Force captured many Germans while defend-
ing the Anzio Beachhead in southern Italy.*

Everything's OK here." Sometimes, however, German patrols
would trip over or spy a telephone wire, and tap into the
conversation. So when Harry phoned and said: "Charlie?"
he was interrupted by: "Ya! Dis iss Charlie!" Harry said
later that he imagined about twenty big, close-cropped
German soldiers gathered around trying to listen in on the
conversation. "Like hell this is Charlie!" he shouted into
the phone, then he and Jerome beat a very hasty retreat
back to our lines!

One day, as we were lying in our foxholes, word filtered
down from headquarters about enemy activity. The report
was that an enemy unit was digging in about half a mile in
front of our lines in a small wooded area. Keeping to the
ditches, about a dozen of us went out to clear out the woods.

I was a little ahead of the rest, as I threaded my way around the bushes and trees. Then the most amazing thing happened! When I came to a small clearing, I was confronted by an enormous snake. It looked to be about eight feet long. I didn't think they had such snakes in Italy. It was rearing up like a cobra coming out of an urn, but its neck wasn't shaped like a cobra's. I was certain that I could blast its head off with a burst from my tommy gun, but I reconsidered, because that might cause my buddies to open fire, and I was in front of them. So I quickly skirted around the snake and let it be.

We combed the entire woods. No Germans. It had been a false alarm. When we got out in the open, the German artillery was ready for us, and shells started to land amongst us. We took shelter in a ditch, but not before one of our men was killed. We decided to leave him and come back that night to carry him out.

That night we brought a stretcher and started to carry our dead comrade down the road. I went ahead as a scout. It was very dark, and I was taken by surprise when I heard an angry command: "Halt!" Of course, I stopped immediately. "Give the password!" I panicked. I'd forgotten the password! My God! Was I going to be shot by my own men? "Wait a minute! Wait a minute!" I shouted. "I forget it, truthfully. I know it! I just forget it! For God's sake, I'm one of you guys, from the first company, first regiment, First Special Service Force!" "Yeah!" was the gruff reply, "And I'm Bob Hope in disguise!" Even in my terror, I wondered whether the Germans would know Bob Hope. Finally, my brain clicked into gear. The word was one we used when we jumped from a plane when we were parachuting. "Geronimo!" I shouted, my voice shaky with relief. "Soft landing," grunted the men from the outpost, as they grudgingly let us pass.

x x x

It was Frederick the Great, in the eighteenth century, who first offered this very sound advice: "Don't fire till you see

The walking wounded — mountains of Italy, January 1944.

the whites of their of eyes!" This was a good plan at the time, since their guns had a very short range, and their battles were fought in the daylight. Our weapons were much more deadly, and we often fought at night, when it was hard to see bodies, let alone heads or eyes. Before long, some anonymous wit had adapted the general's famous advice to fit our situation. Before venturing into the darkness, we'd say to each other: "Don't *wait* till you see the whites of their eyes!"

x x x

Lieutenant Airth was one of our best-liked officers. The men would do almost anything for him.

We were coming back from a night patrol. The sky was just starting to show brilliant streaks of dawn. We were in No Man's Land, on the Anzio Beachhead. It didn't look anything like the unearthly devastation I'd seen in pictures from the First World War. In fact, it was a pastoral landscape. Some of the farmhouses had been destroyed, but many were unscathed.

Although I was exhausted, I couldn't help but be impressed by the beauty around me. The pretty little white farmhouses had their barns attached so that they formed one building. They had been long since vacated, and their inhabitants evacuated to safety. The fields, and the flat land, were covered with gently blowing poppies. They looked like huge red undulating carpets. The size of the poppies amazed me; some were as large as my hand! The beauties of nature always gave me a feeling of peace and tranquillity.

Lieutenant Airth was leading as we trudged through one lonely looking farmyard. Because the barns were attached to the house the manure piles were usually in close proximity. An innocent looking little puddle was blocking our way, and Lieutenant Airth decided to trot through it. It looked to be only about two or three inches deep. The lieutenant stepped into it, and in the flash of an eye he was up to his armpits in cow manure and water. By disturbing the mushy goo, he gave rise to the aroma, and as soon as we got a whiff we decided to distance ourselves.

Lieutenant Airth was really trapped. He struggled to get out, but to no avail. The hole was too deep and the sides too steep and slippery; all his flapping around and struggling got him nowhere. It was then that our beloved officer panicked. He started to yell for help, but, holding our noses, we pretended we didn't hear him. He started to curse and swear and threaten us, but we wanted to get as far from that smell as we could. Then the lieutenant started to plead with us,

and nearly in tears, he reminded us how well he'd treated us on different occasions.

Finally we did what we had to do, but not until Norm Gray, our platoon philosopher, had put in his two cents' worth: "What an ignoble end for such a gallant officer!" So back we went, still holding our noses. We held out a rifle. The lieutenant grabbed it like a drowning man grabbing a piece of driftwood, and we pulled him to safety. What a sorry-looking mess the lieutenant was—soaked and smelly. Not to mention hurt and angry. He cursed us all the way back to our lines—but he had to do it from a *great distance!*

x x x

One night in February, Lieutenant Airth sent Sergeant Flannery and three others out to man a listening post. Besides their telephone and roll of telephone wire, they each carried a machine gun and ammunition. The night was peaceful until about eleven, when the silence was broken by the chatter of machine guns, rifles, and exploding grenades. We listened apprehensively for awhile, and then Lieutenant Airth

112

said, "Let's go see what's going on!" Well, to tell the truth, I wasn't too anxious, but when the lieutenant strode out ahead, two other fellows and I reluctantly followed him.

We had gone only a short distance when the firing stopped. This worried us more than all the noise. Had Flannery and his buddies been killed? Lieutenant Airth felt responsible for his men, so we stumbled along in the dark until we found Flannery's outpost. It was just off the road, concealed in some bushes that were bordered by an open field. We could just make out the outline of the machine gun. It was set up and facing the field; a couple of cans of ammunition lay beside it, but there was no sign of Sergeant Flannery or his men. (We later learned that Flannery's three men had been wounded—one seriously—so he had taken them back to our lines.)

We had little time to worry about Flannery and the others, however, because the enemy suddenly came to life. The night was alive with what looked like fireflies. Would that they had been! In reality, they were tracer bullets coming towards us from the dark field ahead. "Get that machine gun working!" shouted Lieutenant Airth. He needn't have shouted, because I was down behind it when I heard the first shot fired. I started firing in the direction of all the flashes.

It was then that a very strange thing happened—something very uncharacteristic of me. My fear seemed to fall away. I wasn't afraid any longer. Death was the furthest thing from my mind. My notion was that these shadows in front of me certainly couldn't hurt me; and, conversely, these weren't people I was shooting at—I was merely spraying bullets into the shadows! I was filled with an exhilaration I cannot explain. I began to shout above all the noise. My voice didn't even seem to belong to me as I shouted over and over again: "Come on, you German bastards! Come on, you German bastards!" Lieutenant Airth and the others must have thought I'd gone crazy, but probably they were too busy to worry about me.

The enemy seemed to be in a semicircle in front of us, judging by the flashes of rifles and machine guns. During the heavy firing, I saw a distinctive spark of light, at least three or four times. I didn't know what it was, nor did I much care. But the next day, thinking back on the madness, I realized that the sparks had been caused by German machine-gun bullets hitting the front leg of my machine-gun tripod and ricocheting off. But for luck, I'd have had three or four bullets in the chest!

My intoxication ended as suddenly as it had begun. The nearby explosion of hand grenades commanded my attention, making me realize that I was not invulnerable. Then I heard the groans of one of our men who'd been wounded. But what most startled me was that I ran out of ammunition! Holding onto the trigger, I heard the noise of the gun give way to a dull, metallic clank, as the bolt came up against an empty chamber. I reached for a spare box of ammunition, but the box was as light as a feather.

I guess Lieutenant Airth recognized how useless the situation was before I did. He yelled: "The other two guys are hit. Let's get the hell out of here!" I hadn't even thought of retreating, but then I hadn't been "thinking" at all! The lieutenant was right. It was time to save our skins—quickly. We got out as best we could with our two wounded buddies. Panting and puffing, we finally reached our line, only to be brought up short by the challenge: "Halt, who goes there?" Lieutenant Airth pushed to the fore. "It's us!" he gasped. "Men from first company, first regiment!" "That's no good to me!" yelled the challenger. "What's the password?" Lieutenant Airth turned frantically to me, but my mind was as blank as his. Then he screamed at me, although he was only three feet away: "You must know it. They gave it to us just before we left our lines!" We racked our addled brains for a clue, but nothing came to me. As this had happened to me before, I began to think that it was my fate to be shot by my own men for forgetting the password. "It was something we yelled when we jumped from a plane!" Airth screamed. Then one of the wounded men came to our rescue. "Powder River," he whispered between groans. "That's it!" yelled the lieutenant triumphantly. "Powder River! The password is Powder River!" he screamed at our challenger. The soldier on guard instantly came back with the countersign: "Let 'er buck!" Then he graciously let us limp into friendly territory. After getting the two wounded to first aid, Lieutenant Airth and I each went to our own dugouts. I don't know about him, but my exhaustion overruled my frayed nerves, and I fell asleep immediately.

The next morning, Tiny Beacon, pumped the lieutenant for information. "What the hell was all the firing about last night?" "I don't know. I didn't hear anything!" answered Lieutenant Airth. Then he gave me a sly wink. Some sense of humour, I thought to myself. I wanted to forget the whole episode—but I wanted to learn a sure-fire way of remembering passwords.

x x x

Sergeant Gordon and Sergeant Grey argued politics, and they did it the way it should be done—face to face, while straddling a ditch in squat position with their pants down.

On the Anzio Beachhead, in the spring of 1944, they would repair to our rustic toilet and determine with certainty how Prime Minister Mackenzie King and the rest of the dolts in Ottawa could better run the country. Specifically, they took opposite positions on whether labourers in Canada should be allowed to strike during wartime and whether there should be conscription.

Neither was backward in his opinion, and the Germans may have been able to hear them across the three miles of No Man's Land. Their bond of disagreement was as intense and as solid as that of my mortar-crew buddies Tratt and O'Brien. They waved their arms and shouted for interminable periods. They looked precarious; they looked excruciatingly uncomfortable; they looked ridiculous and vulnerable. But they were oblivious. They knew why they were there!

We prayed that they would fall in, but they never did. They were—arguably—the funniest thing I've ever seen.

x x x

After ninety-eight consecutive days on the line, we were taken back to a rest area. Here we were fed some delicious hot food, and got the chance to really relax. The rest-up was in preparation for the breakout from the beachhead and the drive to Rome.

We had been there only a few days when we heard the rumble and clank of tanks. About ten Sherman tanks pulled up in a field just behind our rest area. We were told that we were going to be instructed on how the infantry and tank crews could cooperate in the big push.

We were taught how to mount and dismount the tanks. We also practised advancing with the tanks. We were to walk behind the tanks and use them as a shield against enemy fire. It all looked so easy and seemed to work so well—in theory.

The commander of the tank detachment then got us all together to educate us even further. "Many people think," he said, "that a tank is invulnerable, and that it can just roll over everything and crush you all to death. So when they see a tank coming towards them, they'll jump out of their foxholes and flee in terror. That's a big mistake. The safest place in the world, when a tank advances towards you, is in that muddy little foxhole! Right now we're going to show you that this is true!" He instructed five of us to dig foxholes, which took no time, because the ground was soft.

The other "volunteers" and I then stood looking at him nervously, wondering what came next. He looked us all over, and his eyes stopped on me. He wiggled his forefinger and beckoned me forward. "Now," he said, pointing to me, "the sergeant will demonstrate why it's safe to stay in your fox-hole when a tank is coming towards you." He then told me to get into one of the foxholes. I knew, vaguely, that this would be horrible—terrifying—but I couldn't chicken out, with all my buddies looking on. I had the sense to pick the deepest foxhole. "Get down as far as you can!" came the unneces-sary order. The hole was too short, however, to lie in so I knelt down, and compressed myself as tightly as I could.

Almost immediately, I heard the horrible sound that I'd half expected! One of the Sherman tanks started up, and then began to rumble and clank towards me like a gigantic pulverizer. I remembered the tank commander's awful word, *crush.* The ground shook as that monstrosity came nearer and nearer to where I was crouching with my face buried in the mud. Then everything became very dark. Peeking up, I saw that one of the treads of the tank had completely covered the top of my foxhole. Then its motor shut off. My God, I thought, I hope it hasn't broken down. How long would I have to stay here, shivering in the dark? Thank God I wasn't claustro-phobic!

Then the tank's motor started, and I heaved a sigh of re-lief. That was premature, however, because what happened next was even scarier. The tank's treads started turning, but the beast didn't move! This process began to chew up the grass and mud, which came cascading down onto my shrink-ing form. "What in the hell are they trying to do?" I won-dered. "Don't they realize there's a terrified soldier crouch-ing down here, expecting a tank tread to crush him to bits at any moment? Why don't they stop?" A terrified yell formed in my throat, but my pride just wouldn't let that scream es-cape.

It felt as though that tank sat above me for at least ten min-utes, but I'm sure that the time was much, much less. At last, with a great roar, the steel monstrosity surged forward. At last the sunlight flooded in on me!

With a surge of joy, I leaped out of the foxhole. A bunch of the guys crowded around me. "How was it, Pep?" asked O'Brien. "That must have been scary under there?" "Naw!" I said. "There was nothing to it. It didn't bother me a bit." I tried, as always, to maintain the unwritten code of bravado and denying one's fear that almost every soldier does his best to practise from the day he signs up. But I don't think that we fooled each other very often. This time—as on most such occasions—they only had to see how much I was shaking to know my true feelings.

x x x

We had heard rumours (That was the way common soldiers usually found out what lay in store for them), that the breakout from the beachhead was finally about to begin—on the next day. Major Becket appeared and said that he wanted two groups of radio operators to jump behind enemy lines that night. They were to land on a certain mountaintop from which they would observe the movement of enemy troops. Spud Wright and I were "chosen." "Why me?" I asked, saying that I wasn't a radio man. "We're taking you for your singing, to keep up the morale," said the major. All well and good, I thought, but who's going to keep up *my* morale?

We were taken by boat to Salerno, and that night we loaded into a DC-3 and took off. It was pitch black, but soon I could see little puffs of light, and feel the plane shuddering as the anti-aircraft guns fired at us. We all looked expectantly towards the major and Spud, who was second in command. All we could see was their dark figures. We couldn't see the expressions on their faces or hear them. We saw Spud get up, go to the door of the plane, and look out. We could see the concern on his face as the flash from the exploding shells illuminated it. He returned to where the major was sitting, and they talked in muffled voices. Spud told me the story later. "The major said: 'What do you think, Spud?' So I went to the door and looked out. The shells were exploding all around. I went back to the major and told him it would be suicide to jump in that!" With this advice, the major decided to return to base.

The next day, we heard that the push to Rome had begun without us, and that the First Special Service Force had spearheaded the drive and suffered a lot of casualties. This news made us want to jump because we thought that it might be of some help to the outfit. We strapped on our parachutes and took off again that night. Close to where we were to jump, we flew into another terrible barrage of artillery fire. The plane was buffeted back and forth as shells burst around us. It was decided, again, to abort the mission. We ordinary soldiers had no say in the matter, of course; we did what we were told. Speaking for myself, though, I was in complete agreement. If I was going to die, I wanted a fighting chance. I didn't want to be blown to pieces dangling helplessly from the shroud lines of a parachute. We flew back to Salerno. The pilot told us that because of the darkness and the flak he couldn't guarantee we'd land within five miles of our objective. It was a good thing we hadn't jumped!

We rejoined our unit the next day, and I learned that First company had already suffered many casualties and that my two closest friends, Tratt and O'Brien, had been captured. They, along with a few others, had been cut off by German Tiger Tanks and had no choice—it was surrender or die. We started to advance again, but we came under a very heavy barrage of artillery fire. We recognized the guns as the dreaded "88s." I think this was the deadliest weapon of the war—excluding the atomic bomb, of course. The number 88 referred to the calibre of the gun, which had a shell with a diameter of 88 mms, or about 3 1/2 inches. It was used with devastating effect against aircraft and personnel. In fact, one of the songs we used to sing went: "Those 88s are breaking up that old gang of mine."

These deadly guns had us pinned down, and we dug in,

each man to his own foxhole. Our foxholes formed a rough defensive position, and we settled down to wait out the barrage. We had endured the shelling for some time when a friend of mine, Frank, crawled over and squeezed into my foxhole with me. "I can't stay in there any longer, sergeant!" His face was white as a sheet, and his hands were shaking. I wasn't that calm myself, but I could see that he was in a bad way. For a man to desert his post and thus endanger his comrades—that was almost inexcusable! I reminded Frank of this, and ordered him to get back to his post, but he insisted that I go with him, to see why he had abandoned his foxhole. I couldn't imagine what would scare a veteran soldier into deserting his post, so he and I got down on our stomachs, and crawled the fifty yards or so to his foxhole.

He had dug a "model" hole—about six feet long, two feet wide, and four feet deep. I wish mine had been as nice. But my envy turned to fright, when, with a trembling finger, Frank pointed out a shiny object protruding through the wall of his foxhole. It was the nose of an 88-mm artillery shell! The shell had hit the ground about eight feet in front of his foxhole and knifed its way through the ground until its tip pierced the wall of the foxhole.

I could just imagine Frank's reaction when he heard the shell hit the ground, felt the jar in his foxhole, and then saw the snout of the 88 shell in the hole right beside him. And all this terrific impact without exploding. It was a miracle! It hadn't exploded, but would it explode, and if so, when? I immediately shared Frank's desperate need to get away from this foxhole, so, I told him to join me, and we quickly wormed our way back to my dugout. When we reached sanctuary, we flopped down—exhausted, physically and mentally.

Then Frank looked at me and I looked at him, and we said, as in one voice, "Thank God for the Polish workers!!" We had heard stories that Poles, forced to work in German munitions factories, tried to sabotage the weapons. "Thank God

Easter service on the Anzio Beachhead, 1944.

for the Polish workers!" we repeated. Finally the barrage lifted. We surged to our feet, saddled up, and pushed on towards Rome.

Chapter 17

Even the Best
of Friends Argue Too!

George Tratt and Jim O'Brien stuck together throughout the war—and they argued every step of the way.

They were two of my closest wartime comrades, from the day, back at training camp in Montana, when the three of us and poor, unfortunate Smitty became a mortar crew, until the last time I saw them during the war. When I rejoined my unit after an abortive attempt to parachute behind enemy lines, I was saddened by how much had changed for the worse in a couple of days. The high casualty rate amongst my comrades was shocking, and the capture of Tratt and O'Brien meant the end of our crew.

I tried to make light of it, thinking that at least they were alive, and envisioning them together, arguing with the German Tiger Tanks before conceding the lopsided dispute and surrendering.

x x x

We'd been a pretty good crew. In fact, O'Brien always maintained that we were the best one in the regiment, and who were we to argue with that? However, if Tratt never took issue with that, he seemed to argue with O'Brien about everything else. Maybe it was because Tratt was a Canadian from Montreal, and O'Brien was an American—from Bridgeport, Connecticut. Whatever the reasons, they were the best of buddies until one of them dug up a bone of contention. And what strange bones some of them were!

I remember that when we were living together in big pyramid-shaped tents in the Aleutian Islands, their differences would really get on our nerves. It stayed light up there until 11:30 or midnight, and after a hard day of training we longed for darkness and sleep. O'Brien's voice would break the silence. "Yeah, but if the king was in Canada and stubbed his toe and said, 'Oh, shit,' ten thousand loyal subjects would squat and strain!" Tratt would always take the bait. "Oh yeah? What about you Americans? The Civil War has been over for one hundred years and you're still at each other's throats!" Once started, they would yell absurdities at each other until their voices gave out. Only then would silence return to the muskeg; only then could we sleep. I don't know why we never tried to shut them up, as we had Woodard. Maybe we knew that it would have been impossible!

The only time I remember them being quiet around each other was when they pitted wits in a game of chess. When we sailed from Norfolk, Virginia, to Casablanca, on the luxurious *Empress of Scotland*, we had many hours to while away. Tratt would lovingly remove a small, hinged wooden box from his pack; it unfolded, magically, into a chessboard. In the centre of each square was a neat little hole, into which the pieces fitted. The concentration and silence in these games was even more intense than their noisy arguing. It was scary! We felt that a torpedo could blow us to smithereens and that they'd continue the game—floating away on a piece of driftwood. Their silent competition was just another form of arguing! I never did find out who was superior in chess. As with their shouting, they seemed about evenly matched; and it was never certain where one match left off and the next began.

On our first night in Africa, I retired to the tent exhausted from the ocean voyage—throughout which I'd been seasick most of the time—and longing for sleep, to help me recover my land legs. Tratt and O'Brien, however, commenced a wrangle so pointless that everyone feared that this one would go on forever. When looking at the printed page, do you read

the black or the white? they asked each other. It was their ideal argument—insoluble, useless, silly. They bit into it with such intensity that no one could tell whether they really took themselves seriously. Tratt was on the white side, O'Brien was on the black. "Everyone knows that you read the black letters," shouted O'Brien. "No, no, that's where they're mistaken," countered Tratt. "You read the white around the black letters!" It went on and on, into the wee hours of the morning, and ended—without resolution, of course—after their usual fashion, only when the body could take no more. O'Brien finally rasped: "OK, OK, you win, but only because you can holler louder than I can!"

We had only been on the Anzio Beachhead a few days when Tratt and O'Brien were put on listening post together. During the night we heard a lot of rifle and machine-gun fire, and we couldn't tell where it was coming from. I was worried about my buddies, so I went out to see whether they were OK. Standing in the middle of a road, in the darkness, I called out their names. Tratt called back: "Here we are Pep!"

But then O'Brien piped up. "Are you crazy? He may be a German!" "But he said our names!" argued Tratt. "Anybody could find out our names!" countered O'Brien. "Look out, I'm going to open fire!" Then I really got scared, so I jumped into the ditch for cover. How ironic it would be to be killed by your best friends. I pondered my situation. If they opened up on me in the darkness, would I fire back, or just wait out their fire and pray? I never found out, thank goodness, because as I listened, anxiously, Tratt—with great persuasion, and only after much arguing—finally convinced O'Brien that no other damn fool would stroll down a pitch-black road and yell out their names. So they invited me over to their ditch, where I gratefully joined them—even though they'd scared me almost to death. Their damn arguing ... would it never stop? Strangely, that was the only time I ever heard either of them sincerely concede an argument to the other!

Probably the last time I heard these buddies argue was on the Anzio Beachhead. Our platoon was sent on a night-fighting patrol. We were to clear out some houses believed to be occupied by the enemy. Mortars, being of little use at night, were left behind, and the mortar crew was given a machine gun. Kufta and Frenchie Blanchette had a bazooka, which was often used for house-clearing, because it could easily penetrate the masonry walls. Many of us had rifles loaded with tracer bullets, which the enemy would think were many machine guns.

"Fire a bazooka shell into that house!" ordered Lieutenant Airth. Blanchette loaded the bazooka, attached the wires, and tapped Kufta on the shoulder. Kufta pressed the trigger, and smoke belched from the rear of the barrel as the rocket sped straight to its target, connecting with a resounding explosion. "Give it another one!" yelled Lieutenant Airth. "Load 'er up again, Frenchie!" yelled Kufta excitedly. But Blanchette instead began hollering, "Where are you, Kufta? Where are you, Kufta?" His protective visor—which was standard issue for bazooka crews, to protect them from the smoke their weapon gave off—had gotten steamed up from his breathing, and he couldn't see a thing. Many soldiers refused to wear the visor for that reason. I could hear Frenchie's plaintive cry even above the rattle of the machine gun and the rifle fire.

O'Brien and Tratt, meanwhile, had set up their machine gun where Lieutenant Airth had ordered them to. The rest of the platoon, however, had advanced far ahead of their position; it was, in other words, time for a judgement call, and for Tratt and O'Brien, that meant an argument. So they had one, right then and there!

There were two legitimate courses to consider. O'Brien had orders to stay in one position, and he'd do so, come hell or high water. Besides, he, not Tratt, was in charge of the gun. Orders were orders, and he was a soldier. Tratt, on the other hand, thought that because the rest of us had advanced so far that the machine-gun position wasn't useful, they were being left out of the action altogether. So, picking up his rifle, he started to follow the rest of us.

"Where ya goin'!" shouted O'Brien angrily. "Up where the action is!" Tratt yelled back. "But we got strict orders to stay here, and that's where we'll stay!" "Maybe you will, you old woman, but I'm going up where the action is!" And with that, Tratt joined the rest of us and left O'Brien, fuming, still positioned behind the machine gun.

Their yelling could sometimes be heard, even above the bazooka explosions, above the rifle fire, and above the chatter of the machine guns. If the enemy had heard them, I thought, he'd get a false sense of security, thinking there was great dissension in our ranks.

When I got back to my unit and learned, to my dismay, that my buddies were gone, I realized that there was something worse, for me, than their arguing—the absence of it. Then I felt some pity for the German guards. Their peaceful lives, far from combat and the sound of battle, would be shattered by Tratt and O'Brien yelling, far into the night, "What do you read in a newspaper, the black or the white?"

Some good things, I'm happy to say, continue for a long time. After the war we three often reunited, and I had many opportunities to bask in the heated glow of Tratt and O'Brien's noisy friendship.

Chapter 18
Comrades

They were inseparable! Every minute they could be together, they were together. They seemed to have so much fun—kidding, laughing, joking, singing. Still, they were as opposite as any two buddies could be. Briddon was a short, stocky, rugged-looking individual. You wouldn't call him handsome, but he wasn't ugly, either. I remember he had fairly large teeth, which seemed to become very prominent when he was talking. Briddon looked old for his age, and it's hard to look old at twenty-three.

MacIver was much more youthful-looking. At twenty-one he still looked like a teenager. He was a very handsome and clean cut, and, although he was dressed exactly like the rest of us, he always seemed to be much better groomed. He had a quick, boyish smile, and he was easy to talk with.

If Briddon and MacIver were physically unalike, they had things in common. They both called Toronto home, and they were both very proud of serving with the First Special Service Force. But the most important thing that they shared was the strong bond that too few people experience—the bond of comradeship.

MacIver also had a close relationship with Lieutenant Airth, our platoon commander. The lieutenant, however, was more of a father figure to him than a buddy. Their bond had been forged when Airth had saved MacIver's life by pulling him out of the icy Bering Sea—even though, to do so, he disobeyed strict orders by doubling back to make the rescue. Ever since then, MacIver had regarded Airth as someone to trust and respect; and the young soldier had become almost as a son to the lieutenant—someone to protect and care for.

I can still see Briddon and MacIver's hilarious way of greeting each other. Instead of shaking hands, they'd step to one side, bend over, and pat each other on the backside. "Hi, Briddon!" "Hi, MacIver!" And we'd break up laughing.

I can see them, too, with an arm over each other's shoulder, kicking their legs up like chorus girls. Their moves looked clumsy and comical performed as they were in huge, mud-covered combat boots, but they kept a fairly good time to the song they sang:

> Why don't you do to me
> Like you did to Maria
> Saturday night! Saturday night!
> First you caressed her
> Then you undressed her
> Saturday night! Saturday night!
> Roses were red, red,
> Ready for pluckin'
> Girls sixteen were ready
> For ... high school!
> *A week ago Saturday night!*

This little song-and-dance was always well received by the rest of the guys.

That was Briddon and MacIver, always laughing and horsing around. Whenever I remember them, I think of the ultimate in friendship and comradeship. And they, like the rest of us, in the joy of youth and health, thought that they would live forever—until the hell of an artillery barrage changed our thinking.

x x x

We had been taken off the lines a few days earlier for a much-needed rest. Our rest area was a shallow valley, with a gentle

hill on either side. The valley was only about twenty feet wide, but it stretched for hundreds of yards; it seemed to provide a natural shelter from enemy observation, although we knew that it was well within range of enemy artillery—like every place on the Anzio Beachhead.

We even had entertainment! A Scottish unit from the British Army, resplendent in their kilts and tunics, with a jaunty slant to their Glengarries, had marched up and down the valley in perfect formation to the loud skirl of the pipes and the beating of drums. Canadians and Americans alike became Scots for the day, as we sat together on the hillsides, while the highlanders filled the air with inspiring songs like "The Road to the Isles," "Scotland the Brave," and "Amazing Grace." For the moment, we forgot all about the war.

Ironically, the spectacle that cheered us may have also brought us to the attention of the Germans. They were too far away to hear the pipes, or the clapping and hollering, but they may well have seen the pipe band disappear into our little valley and seen us milling around to get a better view of the show. Hindsight, however, cannot change what happened.

Our officers, too, seemed to have been lulled into a false sense of security. It was hard to imagine our little oasis as anything but peaceful. Nevertheless, many of us had gone to great lengths to "dig in" well. After so long in the army it had become almost instinctive to make ourselves a hole for protection and shelter. Some of us went to far greater lengths to fashion comfortable "lodging" than we would have on the battlefield, where there wasn't time for such niceties. A few dug holes big enough to accommodate two, but most of us were content to be by ourselves. After we'd dug the holes, we cut logs, and laid them across the top. The more serious of us laid them across the top. The more serious of us laid a tier of logs, some branches, a second tier of logs, some branches, a third tier of logs, and more branches. I, for one, knew that only a direct hit on my fortress could hurt me, and the likelihood of that was very, very slim. I was so proud of my snug little home that I'd have been quite willing to wait out the rest of the war right here, relaxing in my underground castle. MacIver and Briddon, being less obsessive and more casual than me, were content to dig more modest foxholes, about thirty yards apart—joking and bantering as they worked.

That night, I crawled into my little fortress exhausted but self-satisfied. I was jolted out of a pleasant dream by a terrific explosion. Had someone stepped on a land mine? My silent question was answered immediately, because two more explosions came in quick succession. Artillery! The explosions continued until they reached an ear-splitting crescendo! I covered my ears with my hands, and curled up on the floor of my shelter. I smiled through my fear. I'd worked hard building a nearly impregnable fortress, and now it was paying off. The shelling went on and on until I began wondering whether I was the only one still alive. I thought that I should go out, and check on the others, but I wasn't that brave or that foolish. When the shelling finally stopped, I stopped. I immediately fell fast asleep!

I awoke the next morning to the sound of voices. "It's a miracle no one else was killed!" "Oh, my God!" I wondered. "Who was killed?" I scrambled out of my foxhole to a scene of utter destruction. The ground was churned up all around our little valley. Three huge canvas water bags (called Lister Bags), which hung from the trees about a hundred yards apart, had been shredded by flying shrapnel. The miracle was that only one foxhole had suffered a direct hit— MacIver's! A tearful Lieutenant Airth explained what had happened: "Somehow Briddon heard that MacIver's foxhole had been hit. He ran out to help his buddy, and a shell landed close by and killed him instantly. He didn't know that MacIver was already dead." As Lieutenant Airth finished his

Lieutenant Bill Airth (killed in action May 23, 1944) was greatly respected and liked by his men.

Ray Briddon (above) and his comrade MacIver were both killed on the same night, during an artillery barrage.

story, he wiped his eyes hastily. It's not easy for a battle-hardened officer to weep in front of his men. But MacIver had been like a son to him, and we understood his reaction.

Our popular lieutenant was himself killed on May 23, 1944.

I've thought of this tragedy many times. Maybe it was fate, maybe it was meant to be. If they were to be killed, what better way than at the same time. But it left us all with a terrible feeling of emptiness.

I will remember these two comrades forever. What greater friendship and loyalty than to give your life for your buddy? Briddon's action always brings to mind the passage from the Bible: "Greater love hath no man than this, that a man lay down his life for his friends."

Still, however noble, however unselfish, however brave, people may paint Briddon and MacIver, I will always picture them with one arm over each other's shoulder, kicking their legs up to imitate two chorus girls, and lustily singing:

> Why don't you do me
> Like you did Maria
> *Saturday night! Saturday night!*

Chapter 19
The Double Miracle

It was a beautiful spring morning. Little did I know, as I gazed out on the Italian countryside, that this was to become one of the scariest days of my life.

Even as I adjusted my pack, put on my helmet, and checked out my tommy gun, war and death, seemed, somehow, far far away. I was bubbling over with a feeling of well being. I was twenty-three years old and in the pink of health. The fields were lusciously carpeted with a great variety of wild flowers, but it was the enormous poppies, blood-red with black centres, waving in the gentle breeze that most stirred me. It was great to be alive on such a beautiful day!

I was overwhelmed by an urge to sing, and the words of a popular song poured spontaneously out of me.

> Oh, what a beautiful morning,
> Oh, what a beautiful day.
> I got a beautiful feelin'
> *Everything's going my way.*

My singing was interrupted by German shells exploding close by, but even this reminder of reality didn't dampen my enthusiasm. My happiness just had to come out, so I kept singing the same chorus, but I quickly added some macabre humour by changing one word of the last line. "Everything's coming my way!" I sang, with a chuckle of self-appreciation. But a quick glance at my buddies, told me that the shelling had snapped them from their reverie and that they didn't appreciate mine. "Singing under shellfire? Has Herb flipped his lid?" was what I read in their eyes. So I shut up immediately, and got down to the job at hand.

There were about twelve of us in the section: we approached a long stone fence, about five feet high, as we advanced towards our planned objective. All of a sudden *two* miracles happened—in the flash of an eye, although to us they seemed to last forever!—an artillery shell—I'd estimate it to have been about seven inches in diameter, and about three feet long—hit the top of the fence. Miracle of miracles, it *didn't explode*! But it continued coming towards us, turning end over end through the air as my buddies and I stood and watched it—paralyzed! My song was forgotten; the beauty of nature was a thing of the past! We just stared at the approaching shell with fascination and fear, as though we had been mesmerized by a deadly snake. We should have scattered and hit the ground, but not a muscle twitched or moved. All eyes were riveted on that huge missile tumbling towards us.

I guess we were all thinking that this was the end. The war was over for us! In fact, everything was over for us! But then, a second miracle happened. The shell came to a thudding stop, about fifty feet from us—and it didn't explode! That broke our spell. We became mobile, scattered and hit the ground. I thought to myself, as I buried my head under some waving poppies, "My God! How lucky can I get? I'll never come this close to death again without actually being killed!"

I remembered, again, the stories about the forced labour in Germany; and although I'm usually not superstitious, I repeated our little prayer of thanks: *Thank God For The Polish Workers!!!*

Chapter 20
The Drive to Rome

It was the first time we'd seen the Anzio Beachhead from high ground. After clinging, precariously, to that narrow strip of land for four months, we had pushed out of our confinement and were scaling the hills that had been held by the Germans. "My God! They could look right down our throats!" Tiny Beacon exploded. We looked back from our new vantage point and shook our heads in disbelief. The entire beachhead was clearly visible. No wonder the enemy had been able to pound us at will with their artillery. How in the hell, I wondered, had we held that beachhead?

But, to our credit, we had; and now we had a clear goal—to liberate Rome. The town of Cori was our first objective. It was perched on the top of a very high hill. I wondered why so many Italian towns were on the top of hills, where it was so hard to build, and where transportation was difficult. I later learned that they were located for defensive purposes. In earlier times, bandits or rebels, or enemy armies, would think twice about attacking a fortified town in an almost unassailable location.

The Germans offered little opposition when we entered Cori. They seemed more anxious to leave from the other end of town; that was OK as far as we were concerned. It must have been noon when a halt was ordered. It was a much-needed rest after a long climb up the mountain in the hot sun.

I had been aggravated for the past couple of hours by a loose heel on my right boot. As I sat down to check it, the heel came off in my hands. I saw a lone Italian, showed him my boot, and tried to explain my predicament. He seemed to understand immediately, for his eyes lit up and he beckoned me to follow him. I fell in beside him, and as we walked he talked excitedly. Of course, it was a monologue, because I couldn't understand a word that he was saying. We soon reached the outskirts of town. All of a sudden I stopped in my tracks. I had made a stupid, unprofessional mistake! In my hurry, I had walked away from my helmet, my pack, and my tommy gun. For a moment, my mind flashed back to the Halifax army camp, when I'd voluntarily given up my weapon. Had I, after all I'd been through, learned anything about being a good soldier? I couldn't answer my own question, but nevertheless I had to make an immediate judgement: should I continue to follow this stranger? Yes, I decided. He looked harmless enough to me, and besides, I still had my combat knife. Of course, I'd never used it for anything but opening cans of food!

We came to an opening in the side of a hill, which was the entrance to a large cave. As we entered, I was astounded to see hundreds of people. No wonder the town had seemed deserted. The townspeople had all fled to this natural shelter to escape the artillery, the mortars, and the machine guns. The cave was filled with smoke from the many open fires where people were cooking their meals. Curious men, women, and children, crowded around us. Since I had no helmet or weapon, they weren't sure which army I belonged to. "Tadisky? Tadisky?" a few of them asked. I was a bit taken aback, both because I didn't want to be mistaken for a German soldier and because they were so casual about which side I was on. It seemed not to matter to them if I was German, American, Canadian, or French. I shook my head vigorously, denying that I was German, then I pointed to my shoulder patch—the red spearhead, with USA and CANADA emblazoned on it. To my satisfaction, they instantly became friendlier and more excited. A few of them shouted, "Canadese Paracatukist! Canadese Paracatukist!"

They offered me food, but I politely refused, thinking that they needed it more than I did. My guide then took me in tow and led me farther into the cave. We stopped in front of a middle-aged man, and my guide explained about my boot heel. The man nodded vigorously, then pulled a shoemaker's last out of the shadows, and in a matter of minutes the heel was securely re-attached. I offered the shoemaker money, but he refused it, with many a shake of his head and many a shake of my hand. What a pity, I thought, that I couldn't speak their language. I'd have liked to have gotten to know all of these people better. I knew that I'd better rejoin the unit quickly, and as soon as I breathed the fresh air again, I realized how smoky the cave had been. I said goodbye to my guide and offered him money, but he steadfastly refused. Then we shook hands, and I jogged back to my unit.

I just made it in time, because they were saddling up to pull out. I grabbed my helmet, pack, and tommy gun, and we left Cori behind. As we got farther into the countryside, habitation became sparse. Now and again we'd come upon a lone farmhouse. We were passing one house in a little valley when Captain Gray beckoned me over: "Take a couple of guys down there and check that place out!" Three of us fanned out and approached the house, with weapons ready. We were about one hundred yards from it when the door was flung open, and a dirty white handkerchief was waved in the opening. Two German soldiers, hands high in the air, emerged cautiously. We beckoned them forward and noticed that each one had a prominent Red Cross band on his arm. They were medical men. We directed them towards our platoon and then went in to check the house. To our surprise, we found two German rifles hidden in a corner. Red Cross men weren't supposed to carry weapons. "So much for the International Rules of Warfare," I thought.

Just then, one of my buddies gave a yell from the floor below. It was a joyous yell, so I figured that it must be something good. Had they found cheese, bread, meat, or money? Those were possibilities that would have excited me. I rushed out and around to the back of the house. There was a door below ground, and I heard uncontrolled laughter coming from inside. I rushed in and saw that it was a wine cellar! There were no *bottles* of wine here; there were two gigantic wooden casks! They looked to be about six feet in diameter and about six feet long. There was Tiny Beacon, kneeling down and operating the spigot of one of the casks. He had filled his canteen and canteen mug. He had ripped out the lining of his helmet and was joyously filling his helmet with the rich red liquid. Bradley quickly followed suit at the other cask. Then they rushed up to tell our platoon the good news.

Army discipline broke down immediately! Captain Gray watched helplessly as his men descended like a horde of locusts on the farmhouse. Eventually, the captain gave orders to camp there for the night. He had no choice really, because he couldn't have stopped the orgy if he'd wanted to, and the attempt would have made him unpopular. The truth was that a platoon of drunk, uncontrollable men is of little use to any army. To the captain's credit, he knew when to give his men some slack; and that's probably why they obeyed him when he had to restore order.

It was a wonderful, happy night for most of the men. They drank themselves into a stupor and then collapsed on the ground to sleep it off. The few of us who didn't drink were still under army discipline. It fell upon us to stay awake all night and stand guard. Who were the clever ones, I wondered? The rest of the guys sure looked as though they had much more fun, but I had made a personal pledge, early in army life, that I would never touch liquor. Now I was paying for that pledge!

It was hard to start marching again the next morning. Most

of the men who had drunk a lot had terrible hangovers, and we sober ones were tired after standing guard all night. But discipline was the order of the day, and move we did!

As we got closer to the enemy, their artillery fire became heavier. We were wending our way through a beautiful olive grove when they really zeroed in on us. The shells came in thickly, and we looked frantically for cover. Luckily, there was a frontline clearing station. These were usually very makeshift stations, poorly equipped. To us it was sanctuary, and we rushed towards it.

As we hugged the outside wall of the hospital, someone yelled, "Crane got hit!" "Where is he?" someone else asked. "Up in the olive grove!" Without thinking, I threw off my pack, threw down my tommy gun, and rushed back to the olive grove. It was one of the few times during the war that I didn't think of myself first. All I could think of was Crane, lying there wounded, with shells bursting all around him. I found him lying on his side, curled up. He was unconscious but still breathing. As gently as possible, I lifted him onto my shoulder and headed for the hospital. The shells busting around me speeded me on my way.

Only when I had put Crane on one of the makeshift cots, and left him to the care of the doctors did I start shaking. Such an obvious display of nerves embarrassed me, so I tried to hide it from the others. That's how we usually dealt with our fear in the army.

Chapter 21
Bravest of the Brave

People have often asked me what it felt like to be in battle. No two times were the same, but the experience was so horrifying that it awakened in me a sense of betrayal. I began to realize that throughout much of my boyhood I had been indoctrinated with the values of patriotism, nationalism, and a willingness to fight and die for my country.

Why else did we have so many poems about war and heroic deeds in our school books? Why were we exposed so much to such poems as "The Charge of the Light Brigade," "Horatius at the Bridge," "The Canadians at Ypres," and "The Revenge"? Why were we, as early as grades one and two, required to recite our allegiance to the flag and to a king who was little more than a picture on the wall?

It is a cliché that when you're in action, many things become clearer to you than they once were. It troubled me that, even as children, we were being indoctrinated into becoming proud "soldiers of the king." What became clear to me, in action, was what it really meant to be a soldier. As my buddy Bradley told the military psychiatrist: "I didn't know that so many guys on the other side would be shooting at me and trying to kill me!"

I had many different feelings in battle. In the first place, I always became very nervous when told that we were going to go into action, and I would begin to shake uncontrollably. I was ashamed of this, and always did my best to conceal it from my buddies.

Once we were in battle, especially if we could see the enemy, my nerves were very steady, and my mind was clear and alert. I was so active that I rarely had time to dwell on personal safety, and I would do things that I never thought I was capable of doing—like carrying to safety a wounded comrade while under fire.

Enduring an artillery barrage was an entirely different and utterly terrifying experience. While under artillery fire, I felt exposed, helpless, vulnerable. There was no way to combat this terror. Guns as much as three miles away were blowing your buddies to hell. You felt trapped. There was no place to run, back or forth; one place was just as dangerous as the other. The only thing to do was to stay put and pray. And when I became a section leader, my men were always looking to see my reaction to the bombardment. My hardest job was to try to appear brave and calm when my heart was thumping wildly in my chest and a little voice deep inside me was crying like a baby.

If we hadn't been buddies and comrades, we probably would have all fled in panic. Each man depended on his buddy. The mortar crew needed four men; the machine-gun crew needed four men; the bazooka crew needed at least three men. We depended on one another for our very survival, so we trusted one another. As comrades, we would never let each other down.

Yes, I was terrified, and although we hardly ever talked about it, each of us knew that we were all terrified. Still, we had been through the horrors of war, together, and we would stick together as long as we could—as long as we were alive!

x x x

Loneliness can overcome you in many different ways. If you are thousands of miles from home, this painful longing is likely to bother most at a time of family celebration, such as Christmas. The mind wanders easily back to happier times: the family gathered around a gaily decorated tree, opening gifts; sitting down to a beautiful Christmas dinner. The warmth of belonging to a family is sorely missed at times. This nostalgic loneliness can flood over you even when you're amongst hundreds of soldiers, many of whom are close friends. My worst attack of loneliness, though, occurred when I was physically alone and in mortal fear. It was a longing, not for home, but just to have another human being close to me—to know that there were other human beings alive in this vast world.

x x x

It was the spring of 1944. The Special Service Force was spearheading the drive to liberate Rome from the Germans. As we were clearing out a machine-gun nest, one the men said to me, "I'm hit, sergeant!" He pulled up his jacket and shirt, revealing the strangest wound I'd ever seen. The bullet had made a shallow groove from one side of his back to the other. It looked as though someone had hit him with a whip! He was very lucky, because had the bullet gone any deeper, it probably would have shattered his backbone, and crippled him. We had been warned about how quickly infection could set in, so, no medics being handy, I practised some crude first aid. We all carried sulfa powder to prevent infection, so I poured some on the wound. Then I told him to go to the rear for treatment.

As he jogged away, I turned around and found myself alone. My platoon had moved on without me. I pushed my way through some bushes and found myself in an empty field. The field was covered with the green grass of spring and a multitude of the huge, blood-red poppies that seemed to grow everywhere. I couldn't resist stooping down to pick one of these beautiful flowers, and as I straightened up, an artillery shell burst in the field about one hundred yards from me. I hit the ground and waited, praying that it had been a stray. No such luck! The shells started coming faster and faster, some closer, some farther away. I felt earth and sod raining down on me. I grabbed handfuls of grass, trying to dig my way into the ground. I wished that my helmet was big enough for me to get under it!

It's much easier to pretend you're brave when your comrades are around you. When you're alone and expecting to be killed, there's no one for whom to pretend. That's loneliness! You can yell, scream, or cry, but no one will hear you. So of course, I did none of those things. I remained silent, not out of bravery, but from terror—and loneliness. I didn't want to die! When you're twenty-three years old, healthy, and love life, who wants to die? And then I had my loneliest, saddest thought of all. What if a shell landed so close that I was blown to bits? No one would know what happened to me. My parents would get word from the War Department that I was missing in action, and that would raise false hope that I was still alive. They might live with such hope for many years. At this, I wanted to howl! These were some of the thoughts that flooded my mind as the field was churned up around me.

The shelling ceased as suddenly as it had begun. A deathly quiet settled over the tortured field. I peeked up from under my helmet, scarcely daring to believe that it was over. It couldn't be true! I didn't have even a scratch! I was covered in mud, and shaking a lot, but I was alive.

I hurried after my platoon and found everyone resting in a convenient ditch. I was among my buddies again! I was alive! I had my whole life stretching out before me! It was a great, great feeling.

I settled down in the ditch, out of breath, and sweat soaked, but I wasn't given much time to relax. "Where the hell you been?" shouted Lieutenant Airth. "I got held up back there!" I shouted back. This seemed to appease him, and he didn't question me further. But my friend Tiny was more persistent. "Were you back there where all that shelling was going on?" "Yes!" I said, as calmly as I could, hoping that he couldn't see how much my hands were shaking. "It sounded to me," said Tiny, "that all hell broke loose. That was one of the worst shellings I've ever heard. It must have been awful to be in the middle of it!" By this time, however, I had recovered my bravado, and I gave the answer that we always gave each other. "Oh, it wasn't that bad!" But I had to bite my trembling lip as I said it.

x x x

Of all the courageous men in the First Special Service Force, the bravest, by far, were the medics. Their duty was to treat and comfort the wounded while under fire themselves. Denied the security of any weapon, they toiled in the front lines through every action.

Two of those brave men who come to mind, were "Doc" Kessinger, from Nebraska, and K.D. Wilson, from Lynn, Massachusetts. I knew these two men because they were in the First Regiment, my regiment. Throughout an attack, they were always closest to the firing; while shells were exploding and machine guns chattering, they were out in the open; while we scurried for cover, they exposed themselves to enemy fire, in order to treat the wounded. They would calmly patch wounds, apply tourniquets, give morphine, and try to make the wounded men comfortable. They made sure that the wounded were carried back to our medical officer, Major Neeseman, as soon as possible.

I remember that K.D. Wilson was furious when he was told he had been "chosen" to be a medic. "I'm a fighting man; I've been trained to be a fighting man; I want to be a fighting man; the last thing I want to be is a pill-pusher!" He did not accept the order graciously, but he learned to understand the importance of his job, and became, in my opinion, the best medic in the unit. Many, many men in the First Special Service Force owe their lives to K.D. Wilson and the other medics.

These were the men who deserved the highest of honours and the most medals; for when you were wounded, frightened, suffering, and lonely, a medic would jog up to you,

Red Cross medic K.D. Wilson has supplies secured. The medics, the bravest of the brave, unarmed and burdened with supplies, ventured into the midst of crossfire to treat the wounded.

and through the noise of the battle you'd hear, "Where ya hit, soldier?" Then you felt safe. You felt that someone cared.

Not only were they the bravest of the brave, but their courage was expressed through saving lives, not ending them. They should have received the praise, the awards, the honours!

I still struggle to understand the nature of fear and courage, mostly by trying to understand those feelings in myself—how they overwhelmed me throughout the war. The medics remain, for me, the model of bravery, and I continue to ask myself: "How could they be so brave?"

Chapter 22

"Ticket Home"

The morning was warm, and although the sun hadn't yet risen, the sky was clear and gave a promise of a beautiful day. A slight mist rose from the warming earth, exposing our foxholes—dozens of them—dug indiscriminately into the Italian countryside. The musky smell of new-turned earth permeated the air.

The tranquillity of the dawn was shattered by the bellow of Captain Gray: "Let's get at it!" We gradually came to life, folding our blankets and groundsheets. Tiny Beacon and I had shared a foxhole. It was nice to have company, especially if you were being shelled. Harmless-looking puffs of white smoke billowed up from a hill in the distance, where artillery shells were exploding and creating an inferno.

Tiny Beacon, from Nanaimo, B.C. was the only soldier left in my section who'd been with me since training. Tiny's stature did not belie his nickname, but what he lacked in size he made up for in guts. Wounded three times in action, he seemed to bounce right back. He was short, stocky, enthusiastic, and energetic. His ruddy face and light blue eyes were topped off with a shock of close-cropped curly brown hair. He complained often, which was normal for a veteran, but he was a dedicated soldier.

Word was passed along that we'd move out in half an hour. Tiny and I reached into our packs for K rations. Tiny ripped his box open and fished out a small can of cheese, four crackers, a fig bar, and a little envelope of powdered lemonade. "For Christ's sake," he erupted. "Cheese and a fig bar. One to bind you, another to loosen you up!" We laughed appreciatively, as we did at anything that broke the tension of waiting to go into action, then we all went back to our skimpy meals and our own thoughts. I reached into my jacket pocket and fondly caressed the last letter I'd received from Greta. I must have read it fifty times! Home seemed so remote, so impossible.

Many times I'd heard the guys talk jokingly and sometimes very seriously of their "ticket home," meaning a nice little wound—not bad enough to ruin you, but bad enough to have you sent home. I'd always felt left out of these conversations, because I knew that I was never going to be hit. I was the only one of the original thirty-four in our platoon who had not been wounded, even slightly. I was going to go through the war unscathed. That certainly was a good feeling, but it deprived me of that elusive dream of a ticket home.

"Let's go!" Captain Gray yelled, and we surged to our feet, fastened our blankets and groundsheets to our rucksacks, and saddled up. We had checked over our weapons. As section leader, I carried a tommy gun while the others carried rifles and our only major weapon—the machine gun—and two tins of ammunition. Each full section of men had three crews, but our mortar crew and our bazooka (anti-tank) crew, had already fallen by the wayside, and they couldn't be replaced during combat. We were now a "section" of four men—five, including me.

Three of my men—Anderson, Patterson, and Munroe—were replacements. Anderson was a tall, lean farm boy from St. Charles, Minnesota, who had fit in quickly because he listened and tried to learn. He was blond and one of his big front teeth was dark, as if he'd gotten hit on the mouth at one time. He was twenty-one, and Tiny and I looked on him as a kid brother. Patterson, on the other hand, was a mousy-looking guy who could always find something to

Tiny Beacon and I served together from training until I was wounded in in Italy. What he lacked in size he made up for in guts. Tiny was wounded in action three times.

bitch about. Munroe was very young, but like Anderson he was cooperative and wanted to be a real soldier.

Our immediate objective was a hill about two miles away, which overlooked the town of Velletri. Our major objective was Rome. Rome! The name conjured up images of "The Eternal City" from my schoolbooks. Our intelligence had informed us that the city was intact although the surrounding countryside was pocked with bomb craters and shell holes. I visualized Rome as a pearl, nestled within an expanse of desolation; and I imagined myself trudging over the cobblestones, (if they had cobblestones), with friendly people waving and shouting and cheering. A hero's welcome, whether I rated it or not!

x x x

We were trudging along single file, and as I looked left and right, I could see many files of troops converging on the hill that we were to take. We reached the base of the hill, without coming under much fire. Snipers off to the left were shooting at us, but they were either out of range or bad shots, because they weren't hitting anyone. Nevertheless, we would all duck instinctively, whenever we heard the whine of a bullet. "You'll never hear the one that gets ya," said Patterson, with the tone of a melancholy two-bit philosopher.

And then all hell broke loose. Three or four machine guns opened up on us, and we could hear the sharper crack of rifles and the unmistakeable bursts of the German burp gun. Mortar shells started landing to our rear, and a creeping barrage began inching towards us. "Another godamned snafu," Patterson grunted sarcastically, as we dove for cover.

"Let's get the hell up there!" bellowed Captain Gray. "You can't win the war lying on your guts!" At times like these, gung-ho officers were really a pain in the butt! We got the point, though, and we started up the hill, crouching as low as we could. Plentiful shrubs and bushes gave us some shelter, and most of the fire was aimed at the column on our right, which had advanced farther than we had.

Our movement left the mortar barrage behind, so we had something to be thankful for. Tiny and I were ahead of the rest of the section, because they were lugging the machine gun, tripod, and boxes of ammunition. A clump of bushes to our right suddenly yielded up two German soldiers, their arms overhead, yelling: "*Kamerad! Kamerad!*" We would have never known they were there if they hadn't shown themselves! They were camouflaged, even to their helmets. One was only a little bigger than Tiny, and the other was about my size. They both looked very frightened, and kept saying, "Austrians! Austrians!" and pointing to themselves. Tiny grunted: "They may be Austrians, but they're all goddamned Germans as far as I'm concerned!" We had no time for ceremony, so we searched them for weapons, then directed them back towards our lines. We couldn't spare guards. We watched them as they trotted awkwardly down the slope with their hands above their shoulders.

Just then we heard a shout to our left from one of the other companies: "They're pulling out! Let's get up there!" We hurried to the top of the hill as the Germans abandoned it. This was our planned objective, so we started digging in. We knew from experience that "Jerry" usually counterattacked as soon as possible, to catch us off balance.

We'd just finished digging our foxholes and positioning our machine gun when someone yelled: "They're coming up!" I rushed to the slope of the hill, and I could see the camouflaged figures darting from one clump of bushes to the other. We figured that they were fresh troops sent in to recover lost ground. Usually, retreating troops provided covering fire for the relief troops. Our hill was surrounded by other hills, some larger some smaller, and in the valley, down to the right, we could see the town of Velletri. There was a large hill directly to the north, about five miles away. At our briefing, Captain Gray had said that we'd be able to see Rome from there.

Tiny and I thought we'd better go down the face of the slope in order to see the enemy better and have a better field of fire. While he went back to get the machine gun, I took his rifle and worked my way down the face of the hill. I fired a few shots, but I didn't expect to hit anyone because the cover was pretty good, and it's hard under any conditions, to hit a moving target at four or five hundred yards. Out of the corner of my eye, I saw puffs of smoke over to my right from a hill higher than ours. I wondered who held that hill.

Suddenly, I felt that familiar feeling—vulnerability, isolation. I couldn't see a friendly uniform in sight—only the scurry of the camouflaged enemy below coming slowly towards me. Then I remembered the identification bracelet my mother had sent me about six months before. On the face of the bracelet was my name and serial number, but the inscription on the back was enough to alleviate all my doubts and fears. "Only The Good Die Young. Love Mum." I felt protected as I fondly touched the bracelet.

I heard Tiny and the others setting up the machine gun behind me. I heard them cursing the war, cursing Hitler, cursing Mackenzie King, and cursing Colonel Ralston (Canada's minister of defence). I knew that the machine gun would soon be opening fire on the advancing Germans. I heard the ammo belts coming out of the box; I heard the clip open, then shut; I heard the bolt being pulled back, and its resounding click. Thank God! The machine gun was ready.

But joy was short-lived. I heard the splat of a bullet hitting flesh and felt a terrific smash on my right thigh, as though someone had swung a big flat board and hit me with all their might. It didn't hurt, it just numbed. My God! What had happened! I'd been hit! What with? I couldn't tell. I rolled over to look, but I dreaded what I'd see. I knew the wound was high on my thigh, because the entire area was numb. Had I lost my manhood? Please God, not that!

My rifle lay forgotten; the enemy was forgotten; my entire concentration was directed towards my wounded leg.

I twisted around to get a better look. My pantleg was quickly becoming saturated with blood. I had thought my blood would be a brighter red, but it looked quite dark. Maybe that was because of the dark khaki background of my pants. I knew that an artery hadn't been severed, because the blood was just oozing out, not coming out in spurts with every heartbeat. I was thankful for that. I wouldn't need a tourniquet, anyway.

I could picture, in my mind's eye, the reaction at home when the got the news. My brother Bill, age nine, would be running around the neighbourhood, shouting, "Herbie got wounded! Herbie got wounded!"

Just then someone bent over me. It was George Wright, a friend of mine from the second company—the same George who'd been so guilt-ridden when he'd visited me in jail. "Where ya hit, Pep?" Before I could tell him, I heard a machinegun chatter and watched in horror as George's web belt and pouches seemed to explode in four different places, as bullets perforated them. He grunted and pitched forward on his face. I dragged myself to him; he was unconscious, and breathing very hard. He had stomach wounds, and I couldn't do anything but pour some sulfa powder on the gaping holes, to help fight infection. I yelled for a medic, which touched off the same appeal from many voices. For a while, all you could hear, from different parts of the hill was: "Medic! Medic! Medic!" It must have sounded like music to the enemy!

Two medics arrived, one carrying a collapsible canvas stretcher. One of them examined me while the other looked at George. He quickly sliced off the leg of my pants and long underwear. I screwed up my courage and looked at the wound. The bullet had entered the outside of my upper thigh, and come out through the inside of the thigh. The hole where it entered was small and neat, but where it came out my flesh was ragged and bruised. Thank God! The wound wasn't high enough to ruin me. I realized then that sweat was pouring down my face. Looking at my wound had been a terrific strain on me. I'll be able to marry! I'll be able to have children! My God, I was thankful! The medic cleaned the wound and bandaged it, then he said: "We'll have to take this guy. He's in worse shape than you. We'll be back in about three hours."

I rolled over and thought about my situation. The chatter of our machine gun gave me a feeling of security. I'd really been hit! And I'd been sure that would never happen. Just then Anderson scrambled down to me. "Can you move—I mean walk?" I said I'd try, but my leg and hip were numb, and I felt I couldn't control my leg. With Anderson's help, I somehow struggled up to the top of the hill, and he assisted me into my foxhole.

"You got it! You got it! You got it!" Anderson kept saying. "Yes," I said, thinking he was saying it in sympathy. Then I realized that he was elated. "Got what?" I asked. "Your ticket! Your ticket!" he yelled. "What are you talking about? What ticket?" I was in no mood for riddles. "Your ticket home, for gosh sakes!" (He never swore.) "Your ticket home!"

The firing increased, so Anderson tossed me his water canteen and rushed back to the machine gun. I lay on my back and gazed at the sky, which had taken on a beautiful deep blue colour and looked peaceful, despite the chaos around me. My mind focused on one thing. Home! I'd actually got my ticket home!! That thought sustained me.

Chapter 23
Naples

"Rome Falls to Allies!" "Allied Troops March into Rome!" announced the headlines of *The Stars and Stripes*—the American army newspaper. I was crestfallen. I'd only been in the hospital near Naples for a few days when the Allies entered Rome. My unit and my buddies had been the spearhead—and I wasn't even there! I was elated for them and bitterly disappointed at the same time. It had been my dream since childhood—when I had learned a little in school about its history and its heroes—to visit Rome. And now I had missed my chance to be a part of the triumphal entry through the gates of the Eternal City.

Indeed I suffered a double disappointment: my "ticket home" was abruptly cancelled when the doctors decided that my wound wasn't serious enough for that; nevertheless, because it had taken so long to remove me from the field, the wound had become infected, and for a while they weren't sure that my leg could be saved. It took me five months to recover, and by then I was going stir-crazy. Even after my wound had healed, the doctors thought that I wasn't ready for combat duty. They said that they'd keep me for a couple more weeks.

The hospital was perched on a high hill, overlooking the city of Naples and it's beautiful harbour. Across the harbour towered Mount Vesuvius. Smoke continually billowed out from its cone-shaped peak. In peacetime, before the American army took it over, it had been a tuberculosis sanatorium.

After five months, though, even physical comfort and the

beauty of nature got monotonous, and the city spread out below was like a siren song to me. As well, I needed to get away from the grim realities of the hospital. After every Allied advance, the wards, and even the halls, were overflowing with casualties. I dreaded seeing the look on the faces of the young men when they found out that would lose legs, or arms, or that they would never see again! I dreaded the smell of chloroform and antiseptic. It seemed that I could even taste the antiseptic in my food, because the smell of it was in my nostrils continuously. I dreaded the groans and moans of the wounded, as they struggled to get some rest in the darkened ward at night.

During my last month in the hospital, I made a new friend. Perkins and I hit it off as soon as he was admitted to our ward. We took to playing cribbage and checkers, and we had enjoyed long talks about plans for after the war. Perkins was from the southern States, and his slow drawl fascinated me. For all the time that we spent together, I never knew what Perkins looked like. I never saw his face, because he was covered in bandages from the neck up. My poor friend had been trapped inside a burning tank and was lucky to have gotten out alive. There were slits in the bandages for his eyes, his nose, and his mouth. The doctors told him that he'd have to endure these bandages for another month. I would be discharged within two weeks, so I'd never, ever see the face of my newfound friend. That bothered me.

The hospital office officials and staff did their best to keep up our morale by providing entertainment. Boxing matches were held in an outdoor ring every two weeks, and I was lucky enough to be at ringside when the great Joe Louis refereed one of the fights. There were frequent movies and stage shows, but after a while, the only thing that I could get excited about was the thought of being free to roam the streets of Naples.

I became determined to get a pass to the city that lay so

invitingly below the windows of the hospital. I was paraded before the officer in charge of our section of the hospital, so that I could request a pass. I was wearing pyjamas, robe, and slippers, but I came to a smart halt at his desk and waited for him to speak.

"What can I do for you?" he asked gruffly. "I'd like a pass to Naples, if it's possible, sir." "It isn't possible," he snorted. "I'm just not permitted to give a leave to a patient of this hospital. A combat soldier must return to his camp before he can apply for leave." After being dismissed by this unfriendly and unsympathetic officer, I did some hard thinking. Getting a leave when I got back to camp seemed an unlikely prospect. My rebellious determination to be my own master (if only for a short while) resurged, and I decided that I'd have to find my own way to get out and see Naples.

Going AWOL from the hospital meant getting a uniform. I couldn't walk out in my pyjamas, robe, and slippers, and I didn't have access to my own uniform. I had become good friends with one of the ward-boys, Corporal Haines, and after a great deal of persuasion, he lent me his uniform. He was smaller than I was, but I managed to squeeze into his clothes. Being a sergeant, I was suffering a demotion by wearing his uniform, but I'd lost my stripes before for going AWOL, so I figured that if I were charged this time I could say that I'd already demoted myself.

I had little trouble getting past the guard at the gate, but I knew that I'd have to steer clear of the military police, because I didn't have a pass to show them. As always, freedom was like several deep breaths of fresh air to me. I just walked the streets, savouring the aimlessness. People were casually strolling, and everywhere there were children laughing and playing. After the army, this was heaven.

Come nightfall, I had to find a place to sleep. As I walked down a very narrow alley between streets, a flashlight came on behind me, and a gruff voice shouted: "Halt! Stay where

The author (second row, right) on crutches recouperating from wound, Naples, Italy, 1944. "It took me five months to recover and by then I was going crazy."

you are, soldier!" I glanced around quickly and saw two MPs, standing by their jeep. They were both wearing sidearms— the regular American Army issue, a .45-calibre pistol. I didn't want to return to hospital yet, so I kept walking. "Halt or we'll fire!" was their response. I must have been feeling very perverse, or brave, because I hastened my retreat. If they handled a .45 like I did, I thought, I was in no danger at all. I was soon on the next street, not a shot had been fired. Thank God the alley had been too narrow for the jeep. I hurried down many streets to make sure I'd lost the MPs.

A short time later, I came upon a bright, well-lit building. It was a military police headquarters. "Maybe I could get a bed here for the night" came the inspiration. It was the last thing they'd expect. I chuckled to myself as I strolled in—

trying to seem offhanded. "Do you have a spare bed for the night?" I asked the sergeant at the desk. "Sure," he said, with a friendly smile, "Harry's on patrol all night. Take his bed over there in the corner." He didn't seem to find my request strange at all. Maybe I wasn't the first soldier to have made it. I thanked him, gratefully, but began wondering whether Harry had been one of the guys who had challenged me in the alley. I put this out of my mind, however, pulled the blanket up high, and had a wonderful sleep.

I got up and out of there early, just in case Harry should arrive and recognize me. I bought a breakfast of coffee (no milk!), black bread, and cheese. The cheese didn't taste half bad, but the rest of the meal wasn't to my taste. Back on the street, I suddenly became terribly lonesome. There were many people around, but I didn't know any of them. At the hospital, I thought, I knew lots of people. I never thought I'd want to go back, but there it was. I guess that my appetite for freedom had been satisfied; what I craved now was company.

I wasn't back in the hospital an hour, before I found myself confronting the same officer who had refused me a pass. "Maybe you're in better shape than I figured," he said. "We'll have to get you back to your unit as soon as possible!" He was as good as his word. The next day, I was transferred from the hospital to a rehabilitation centre in the town of Caserta.

Chapter 24
AWOL to Rome

By now I had nearly recovered, and so far as the army was concerned that meant I'd soon be ready to rejoin my unit, which was stationed hundreds of miles away in southern France. Rome, on the other hand, was enticingly close—only 120 miles away. Yet as each day passed it grew less likely that I'd ever see the fabled city of my boyhood fantasies. That was unthinkable—intolerable—to me. The more I thought about it the louder and more insistent grew the music of my own piper, while the call of duty faded. It was now or never I decided!

I tried to do it the "right" way, although I wasn't very hopeful. Just as I had done while in hospital in Naples, I went to the commanding officer and asked for a pass; just as I expected, he looked at me as though I'd committed high treason, and then he shouted: "Impossible! Not a chance! There's a war on, you know!" I thought that phrase had been worn out long before. "My job," he continued, "is to whip you people into some kind of shape so you can again contribute to our war effort!" Big deal, I thought, but as usual I kept my thoughts to myself while in front of a commanding officer. However, I did get the last word in. "Yes, sir!" I said briskly, then wheeled around and left.

I next approached the sergeant-major, who was more sympathetic, but he could only recommend me for an overnight pass to Caserta, the town five miles away. I was given the pass, which stated that I must be back to camp by eight the next morning. The army truck dropped about fourteen of us off in the town square of Caserta. The others immediately took off in different directions, leaving me alone to make my decision. Was it to be Rome and adventure or an immediate return to my unit, with the likelihood that I'd never by in Italy again? Thought about that way, it was an easy decision. I would seize the chance of a lifetime, even at the risk of severe punishment. That was a real possibility, because I was in a war zone, where being AWOL could be looked upon as desertion—a very serious charge. I hardly gave it a second thought, however. I headed for the main road and in no time was riding all alone in the back of an army truck. Hitchhiking, for an Allied soldier in Italy, was very easy at that time.

It was a dreary autumn day, but I was thinking only of my destination. As we neared the city, I looked around the canvas side of the truck and I saw that we were approaching a huge stone gate that looked at least a thousand years old, and as though it had once been part of a huge fortress that repelled invaders. Then I saw a roadblock. My historical imagination withered; my hopes faded; my blood ran cold!

Six military police were standing there, checking each vehicle. The truck had already stopped, so there was no chance of escape. My visit to Rome was about to be nipped in the bud when I had reached the very gates of the city! Many would-be conquerors of Rome had shared this frustration, I thought. I had no choice but to brazen it out. One MP came to check the back of the truck, where I sat alone on the long wooden bench. "Your pass, soldier!" I handed him my pass for Caserta. He looked at it for a little while, and then, with a shrewd glint in his eye, he said, "Do ya think you'll make it back in time?" "Oh, yes, definitely," I said, but we both knew that I was lying. The MP waved us through and I heaved a sigh of relief. If I'd ever received a break in the army, this was it—and from a despicable MP, my natural enemy!

Rome was all that I'd imagined and dreamed. What splendour! What historic sights! To walk through the streets was to relive the Caesars, the early Christians, the Legionnaires. At home, we were impressed if buildings were one hundred years old. Here they were one and two *thousand* years old! To a boy from a small town like Truro, whose tallest structure was four stories high, it was a sight to behold. The architecture of The Pantheon was magnificent, but it was the Coliseum that most captured my imagination. The central arena was enormous, and the entire edifice was constructed of huge stones piled one atop the other. Even the spectators' seats were made of stone. Boyhood stories flooded back. Here was where gladiators fought to the death and Christians were sacrificed to the lions. I learned that sometimes the whole arena had been flooded so that sea-battles could be held! It was hard to imagine such a spectacle, even considering how much smaller ships were at that time. I sat for a long time on one of the stone benches, and tried to conjure up all of the spectacles—most of them bloody—that I knew had been held here.

I walked around the entire outside, and at one alcove I gave in to that almost universal impulse—I picked up a rusty nail and scratched into the stone wall the initials "G.M." and "H.P.," (Greta MacPhee and Herb Peppard). In some way, I was now part of the history of the place; and maybe—I thought, supestitiously—this was a good omen for our having a future together. I felt quite pleased with that notion as I stepped back and surveyed my handiwork.

I also went to the Catacombs, those long narrow tunnels with the niches in the walls where the dead were buried. A monk held a slender candle attached to a stick; he used this as a pointer while giving us the history of the place in a sing-song voice. He'd memorized his speech, but he couldn't speak English, so it was useless to ask any questions. It was here, more than anywhere else I visited, that the dedication, faith, and suffering of the Christians was forcefully brought home to me. In these caves, dug under the streets of Rome for miles and miles, Christians fled from persecution. They lived, ate, died, and were buried in the damp, eerie confines of those seemingly endless tunnels!

Next I went to St. Peter's Cathedral, where Pope Pius the Twelfth gave an audience to hundreds of us, mostly military people. He spoke to us in Italian, French, Polish, and English. I held up a rosary that I'd bought for my sister, Dorothy, and the Pope blessed it.

I spent seven glorious days sightseeing in Rome. On my first night there, I met a soldier from my own unit who immediately took me under his wing. He worked in supplies, the invaluable section that kept us provided with all our material needs—food, clothing, and weapons. I stayed with him, in his small but cosy room in a building that had been commandeered by the American army. My newfound buddy—I've forgotten his name—scrounged a mattress and blankets, and I gratefully settled in. I picked a corner, spread my mattress on the cement floor and blessed my buddy for providing a safe haven to return to each night.

After taking guided tours to most of the historic sights, I took in some entertainment—a stage show. I went alone, but the theatre was jammed with hundred of raucous soldiers. The place was filled with smoke, and I could see white balloons floating around; but I didn't realize until I saw men blowing them up that they were condoms issued to us by the army. The energy of these men (overgrown boys?) was irrepressible, but basically good-natured. They were, after all, fresh out of combat and greatly relieved to be alive and in one piece!

The show started. Out came "a beautiful tap-dancer from Australia" (according to the announcer). The crowd got even noisier; swearing, and jostling rumbled unabated throughout her performance. Remarkably, a hush fell over the crowd when a matronly-looking woman of about forty came on to sing. She sang the bittersweet German army song, "Lili

Marlene," in both German and English, and her soulful performance brought the house down. By the time she'd finished "White Christmas," there was hardly a dry eye in the place. Swaggering tough guys were transformed into blubbering sentimentalists, and I was no exception. Joining so many of my fellow servicemen in a collective show of emotion proved to be my most memorable experience in Rome. Rarely did soldiers display their feelings, much less share them.

When I left the theatre, I realized that I was getting very low in cash; in fact, I was dismayed to discover that I was down to 288 lire—$2.88. I had no choice but to head back to camp.

I left Rome by the same gate I had entered, but I skirted around the roadblock and walked about a mile before hitchhiking. The first vehicle stopped. It was a command car with a driver in the front and a major in the back. "Can we give you a lift?" asked the major, with a strong English accent. I thanked him and started getting in the front with the driver. "No, no," said the major. "Get in back here with me, I'd like to chat a bit." He did the chatting while I listened respectfully. He had nothing but praise and admiration for the Canadian troops and spoke at great length about their accomplishments on the Eastern Flank, particularly the occupation of Ortona after a very hard battle. He got no argument from me, of course, and I even basked a bit in national pride.

Just then, the vehicle began to slow down and the major asked the driver, "What's up, corporal?" "Roadblock ahead, sir." I was surprised that I didn't much care. I'd achieved my personal objective. I'd spent seven glorious days in Rome, and I was prepared to accept the consequences. The car pulled to a stop. Three military police crowded around demanding identification and passes. The major had little difficulty in identifying himself and the driver; then an MP asked for my pass, and I sheepishly handed him my week-old overnight pass for a town 120 miles to the south. He looked at it, raised his eyebrows, then looked at me, still seated comfortably beside the major. Without a word, he raised his hand close to his face, at about eye level, and with his index finger only beckoned me to step out of the car. I reluctantly left my comfortable seat, and stood on the road beside my captors. The major, although he must have been very surprised, kept his composure, and asked me very politely: "Are you leaving?" I came smartly to attention and said, "Yes, sir!" I later thought that I must have looked ridiculous, under the circumstances.

The staff car drove away. An MP got on either side of me. Each of them were armed with rifles, and as they marched me away, I felt, for the first time since my twenty-eight days in jail, that I really must be a criminal. Not far from the barrier, we came to a halt in front of a small, squat masonry building that looked as though it might house cattle. One MP unlocked the door, which had a small opening at the top with bars across it, and ordered me in. As I heard the door slam and the lock click shut, I took in my surroundings. I was alone; the floor was cement, with some straw strewn over it, and to my great relief, there were two army blankets spread out in the corner over a pile of straw. The blankets were very welcome indeed, because it was the first week of November and quite chilly at night.

By peeking through the bars, I saw that I was on the outskirts of a village. At times local people would pass by on the other side of the street, and at first I waved and yelled: "*Buon giorno*," but they responded with looks of mistrust. It dawned on me that to them I was a criminal—a thief, a deserter, maybe even a murderer! After that I kept to myself, so as not to frighten or embarrass anyone.

I soon became aware of another disconcerting fact: I was not alone in my cell after all. The place was well populated with rats. This didn't bother me much in the daytime, when I was usually on my feet, but it was a different story at night,

when I was lying on the floor. I could hear their continual scurrying through the straw all around me, and I kept my arm across my throat for protection. Despite my nervousness, I eventually drifted off to sleep, and the rats never bothered me.

I spent two days and two nights in this makeshift prison. On the third day, two MPs unlocked the door. "Let's go," they said, and we started to march towards the village. They marched in step, so I defiantly marched out of step with them. Several times they tried to adjust their step so that we'd be synchronized, but I would have none of it. We marched into the commanding officer's quarters all out of sync. I regarded this as a major triumph, but looking back, I think it was a rather pathetic effort to show my contempt for authority.

He was a captain of the American army and he held my wrinkled and crumpled pass in his hand. On the desk in front of him was a piece of paper with writing scribbled on it. He glared at me and said in a too loud voice: "Of course you realize this is a very, very serious offence?" Feeling that he was just stating a fact, and not actually asking a question, I made no reply. He continued: "The area you're now in is regarded as a combat area, and your action could be regarded as desertion in the face of the enemy." I felt colour rush to my face, but still I said nothing. He then blustered in a frustrated tone: "Unfortunately, I cannot mete out your sentence. I do not have the authority to do so. You are a Canadian and you can only be prosecuted according to Canadian Army rules and regulations. My only option is to get you back to your unit as soon as possible, where your own officers can deal with you accordingly." I heaved an inward sigh of relief. At least I'd be tried by people and faces familiar to me.

I was marched from the captain's office directly to an MPs jeep, and with two guards as escorts, we roared southward down the main road. I was told that my destination was the waterfront in Naples. We pulled up at a wharf beside a huge ship with the name "Canada" on the front. I thought that it must be a Canadian ship, but I later learned that it was a French vessel. My two guards walked me up the gangplank to the deck, where I was handed over to two other MPs who would be escorting me and three other prisoners to southern France.

When we left Naples, we prisoners were granted freedom of the ship, because there was no chance of escape. The voyage—as usual—was a nasty one for me. My susceptibility to seasickness was aggravated because the ship was top-heavy—with big guns and armament and very little ballast in the hold—so it was continually rocking and rolling. I thought that the best place to be was up top, in the fresh air. When I got there, I found that many other soldiers had the same idea. We all lay on deck with our feet towards the gunwales.

The night was pitch black, and the ship had no lights because of blackout regulations. When it gave a sudden jerk and listed sharply to one side, I could feel myself sliding swiftly down, feet first, towards the outside of the ship. I came to a jarring stop as my feet hit the narrow strip of steel that rose about a foot above the edge of deck. I felt as though I was half lying and half standing, facing towards the black billowing ocean. The ship teetered there as if trying to decide whether to capsize or return to an upright position. As I dug my back into the deck, and tried to put more weight towards the direction of the cabin, I thought how stupid I was for not having put on my life jacket! I felt that I could almost reach straight out and touch the tempestuous Mediterranean Sea; and if I were thrown into the water in the darkness, there would be no hope of rescue until daylight. Without a life jacket, I'd never last that long. I held my breath as the vessel gave another lurch towards the black waters. I was almost prepared to accept the inevitable, when the *Canada* flopped back to even keel. I lost little time in finding an old "Mae West" life jacket, and strapping it on.

A day and a half later we sailed into Marseilles harbour, at around ten o'clock in the morning. I stood at the railing with the three other prisoners and our guards watching our ship being unloaded. I saw about fifteen German prisoners doing stevedore work on the wharf. They still wore their uniforms, and a German officer gave them instructions while an American MP guarded them all. I saw the officer pick up a piece of old rag, walk behind a pile of lumber, and clean his shoes as best he could. I watched with a mixture of admiration and dismay. The officer was trying to keep himself presentable under the worst of conditions, but he was also trying to maintain the tradition of being a cut above his men.

I was transferred to MPs on shore, who whisked me speedily over the hilly roads of southern France in that versatile little army vehicle, the jeep. But for being under guard, it was a great tour. We drove through the beautiful city of Nice, but we had to bypass Monte Carlo. The principality of Monaco was neutral territory, so it was out of bounds to all troops; nevertheless, we had a wonderful view of its fabulous capital from the cliff that we drove along.

When we reached the town of Menton, on the French-Italian border, I was turned over to my unit's own MP, who quickly took me to our camp a few miles outside the town. The camp was in a small village, and our outfit had confiscated all the houses in the area and was living in comfort. I had a joyous reunion with Tiny Beacon, and many other buddies, whom I hadn't seen for six long and eventful months. My pleasure was tempered, though, when Captain Gray told me that I'd be up on the carpet, in the morning, before Jack Akehurst, the regimental commander.

It was a beautiful morning, but I feared my fate as I was marched into the CO's office. He seemed agitated, undecided, but not overly unfriendly. (After much experience, I could discern, quickly, the bias of my prosecutors.) On this occasion, I think that the strong bond shared by combat soldiers who have served together made the colonel more tolerant of me.

"Peppard," he began, "You have placed me in a very, very difficult situation. There is a charge here stating that you are guilty of going AWOL for several days. That is a very serious charge indeed." I shifted uneasily, wishing that he'd get it over with. "However, I also received information yesterday that you are to be decorated for bravery in action. You are to report to the parade square at 1400 hours, in full dress uniform, to receive the Silver Star from General Frederick." I was flabbergasted. I could hardly believe my ears! I blushed, inwardly, with equal parts of pride and shame. "I have no alternative but to give you a severe reprimand, with grave warning that this sort of thing must not happen again. If you are guilty of any infringement of army rules and regulations in the future, it will go very hard for you!"

I thanked him profusely, and if it hadn't been unmanly looking, I would have kissed his hand. Instead, I saluted, about-turned, and marched away, a free man!

Upon reaching the beautiful outdoors, I twirled around, I ran, I jumped, I shouted! I was deliriously happy. The world was a wonderful place to live in! I was still in the army, but I was healthy, happy—*Free!* I still had to take orders, obey superiors, and do my job as a soldier, but I wasn't going to be thrown into a lousy jail cell!

I had—as usual—no regrets for having followed my own path, which had provided such unforgettable experiences. Deep in my heart, though, I thanked my lucky stars for three men: the understanding MP at the gates of Rome, my buddy in Rome, who had shared his room with me, and Colonel Akehurst, who showed great leniency towards me under the circumstances.

Chapter 25

Breakup!

It was my proudest moment as a soldier—standing in the parade square, amongst my comrades and being presented with the Silver Star by General Frederick, our former commanding officer. My citation was read aloud and the general shook my hand, congratulated me, and pinned the medal on me. I was overwhelmed by emotion and had to fight back tears. I recovered myself when the general spoke to me. "This action happened a long time ago. Why wasn't this medal presented to you before this?" "I was in hospital, sir."

For a short time after that, my unit enjoyed a much-deserved rest on the beautiful French Riviera. The weather was glorious in the late fall of 1944—the days were sunny and comfortable, the nights cool and crisp. Every chance we got, we'd go to Nice by army truck. It was a beautiful drive along a cliff, and we always savoured the tantalizing view of Monte Carlo spread along the crescent-shaped bay below. We lounged in our camp at Menton. This was the kind of "war" I most enjoyed, being in a beautiful country, with hot food, passes to the city and, most importantly—no combat. It was too good to last long!

At first there was just rumours—"latrine rumours," or "scuttlebutt" as we called it. Len Anderson was the first to tell our little group, "I heard the outfit is breaking up." "What in the hell are you talking about?" exploded Tiny Beacon. "That's the craziest damn thing I ever heard! Why would anyone break up the First Special Service Force? The Army's made many snafus but they would never go this far! Why break up a unit that has achieved every task it was ever given? Why break up a winning combination?" I agreed with Tiny wholeheartedly.

But the high command was not motivated by sentiment. It had decided that, with the enemy on the defensive, the Allies had no use for a specialized force of only 2,400 men. What was needed now were divisions, corps, and armies. So our unit must be disbanded.

The final parade for the First Special Service Force took place on a giant field in Villeneuve-Loubet, in southern France. It was a very sad occasion. Some of us had been together since the summer of 1942; now the Canadians and Americans would be separated, perhaps never to see each other again.

The Force flag was slowly wound into its staff, and a case put over it. Then came a command that we'd never heard before and would never hear again. It sounded forbidding and final: "Fall out the Canadians!" We stepped out, leaving many gaps in the line. "Canadians! Form up!" was the next order, and we formed up, facing our American comrades. It seemed fitting that the Americans left gaps in their line, out of respect for their departing comrades. I could see many buddies standing there with sad and reflective stares. I had a great lump in my throat as I fought back the tears. During the march-past we saluted our former comrades, with pride in our shared accomplishments, and we silently vowed that we would never forget them.

Chapter 26

Back to the Canadian Army

A few days later, all the Canadians from our old unit sailed for Naples. From there we were taken by trucks to the camp at Avellino, a big staging area for Canadians. Soldiers returning from hospital; replacements for those who had been killed or wounded; all gathered there.

We were kept in shape by parade-ground training, which was a great aggravation to us combat soldiers. We had to be kept busy, though, because idle soldiers present a discipline problem.

One thing that I'll remember about Avellino is how poor the civilians were. Women carried wood on their heads, down from the surrounding hills. It wasn't stove wood such as we were used to, but spindly branches that obviously wouldn't last long but were probably all that they could get. They wore little more than rags—small protection from the December chill. The children would lie in wait until we finished our meals, then raid the garbage cans for leftovers. We shared what we could with them, but we didn't have that much ourselves. It is, indeed, the innocent, and the weak, who suffer most in wartime.

During our stay in Avellino, I suffered an ironic indignity. I served as an MP! The captain who handed me the armband made it quite clear that I had no choice. Who could be behind such a perverse jest, I wondered, but concluded that I was only getting my just deserts.

When I got back to barracks, my buddies gave me a very hard time. Perhaps I should have tried to hide my MPs armband, but there it was, prominently displayed on my sleeve. Tiny Beacon and Red Pike in particular needled me mercilessly, although Red wasn't so boisterous as Tiny who laughed his head off! "Herb Peppard an MP, Herb Peppard an MP. I've seen everything! The worst criminal of us all is made a policeman." He couldn't stop laughing. Maybe they figure if they make all the criminals MPs, it will keep them in line! "My God, Herb," he went on, "how many AWOL charges do you have against you?" "Not many." I said calmly.

He started to rhyme my misdemeanours off at the same volume. "First there was the time Spud Wright and a bunch of you jerks went AWOL from Fort William Henry Harrison, in Montana. Surely you didn't think you could get 3,500 miles to home, without being caught!" "We hoped we would," I said lamely. "Then before we went to the Aleutians, you took a little sojourn to Montreal. When we returned from the Aleutians, you went AWOL to Nova Scotia for ten days! Major Becket fixed your wagon, didn't he!" "But I didn't think I was going to get home before we went overseas!" I countered. "And I suppose you were heading for home when you took off for Rome, without a leave?" "But if I hadn't gone to Rome without a pass, I would never have seen it!"

"So you feel justified in breaking the law, just to satisfy your personal pleasures?" asked Red Pike. Grudgingly, I admitted that they were right.

But Tiny still wouldn't let me off the hook. "Does the captain who gave you the armband know your record?" "I don't know." "You can be damn sure he doesn't know," snapped Tiny. With a sly wink at Red, he shouted: "All those officers do, is look for the huskiest, stupidest-looking dope, and then they pin an MPs armband on him!"

Being an MP had one redeeming feature: it gave me access to the officers' club, an imposing-looking building on the main street of the little town. I was fascinated and mysti-

fied by the large sign above the entrance: ALLIED OFFIC-
ERS ONLY. I read and reread it, but remained puzzled. In
my mind's eye I saw four German officers strolling down
Avellino's main street, oblivious to the stares they were getting from the soldiers in foreign-looking uniforms. When they
reached the officers' club the Germans stared at the sign above
the door. They shook their heads in disbelief and exasperation. One exploded with: "This is carrying war a bit too far,
isn't it? Just because we're the enemy, we're denied the luxuries of this officer's quarters! We should definitely make an
official complaint to the governors of the Geneva Conference!
This is excessive cruelty, and should not be permitted to continue!" Then they clicked their heels, did a smart about-turn,
and goose-stepped back down the street. As they faded into
the Italian landscape, my mind flipped back to the present,
and I decided to enter these hallowed halls.

I found that what was denied to the German officers was accessible to me, as long as I wore my MPs armband. I strolled into the officers' quarters, and I was overwhelmed by what I saw! There were bedrooms, with beds and bedclothes that an ordinary soldier could only dream of: mattresses, clean white sheets, pillow cases! Investigating further, I discovered a lounge, with chairs and sofas, tables loaded with magazines, and, to top it all off, a bar. Yes, a well-stocked bar, with enough variety of drinks to satisfy any taste. With luxuries like these, officers might prolong this terrible war for years!

But it was the kitchen that most amazed me. The food was plentiful and good; the smell was enough to drive an enlisted man to distraction. In particular, there was a distinctive aroma that I remembered from childhood. As I approached a table, I found that my sense of smell had not deceived me. There sat six steaming hot mincemeat pies! I couldn't believe my eyes. Tiny and Andy certainly wouldn't believe it if I told them, so I thought, why not steal a pie, and take it back to them? As soon as I was alone in the kitchen, I rushed to the table, picked up a pie and thrust it up under my tunic. I strolled out the door at a leisurely pace, so as not to arouse suspicion.

When I reached our barracks, I yelled to my buddies to come share a treat with me. They rushed over as I unbuttoned my tunic. The warm pie and its flaky crust had nearly disintegrated! The portion that hadn't stuck to my tunic dropped in pieces to the floor. This didn't deter my buddies, though. They scrambled to retrieve each delectable morsel, and of course, I joined them. It wasn't quite as I'd planned it, but, as true soldiers, we made the best of it.

A few days later, all the Canadians from the First Special Service Force were called on parade and told what our options were. We were offered the privilege of joining any unit we wished in the Canadian Army—as long as it was in the

European theatre! So much for the rumours that had been flying that we would all be going home as instructors.

Many of us chose to join the First Canadian Parachute Battalion. That was the unit from which I had transferred into the First Special Service Force, so it seemed fitting that I should return to it. Once we'd made our decisions, we were moved out quickly, first to Naples and then, by sea, to England, where the First Canadian Parachute Battalion had its headquarters.

New Year's Day 1945 was spent anchored off Gibraltar, gazing longingly at the shore where we wished we were celebrating. We weighed anchor the next day for the long voyage to Glasgow, Scotland. When we reached the railway station there, we were welcomed by smiling women, who gave us steaming hot tea and scones. Their friendly faces, and Scottish accents were a treat indeed—especially for a Nova Scotian.

We had been told that we'd be going to our unit's camp on Salisbury Plains, but, as usually, the army's logistics had since changed, and we were the last to find out. We ended up, instead at the old army camp at Aldershot. I was struck immediately by the camp gate, with the date 1854 carved into the stone, to mark the Crimean War. What a lot of history there is in this old camp, I thought; what stories these old walls and buildings could tell!

But history and romance aside, the camp was cramped and uncomfortable. We shivered continually while we were in those ancient barracks. Each room was about fifty feet by twenty-five feet and accommodated about seventy men on the usual two-tier bunks. They were almost impossible to heat. There were no stoves—only a small hole in the wall, containing a poor excuse for a fireplace.

We suffered these conditions through most of the chilly, damp English winter, expending most of our energy trying to generate a little heat. To add insult to injury, there wasn't enough fuel. When the coal ran out, we tore up cardboard boxes and ripped up slats of wood from anywhere we could get it. Red Pike and I used to fistfight until we were exhausted. That was probably the best means devised of keeping warm—and we got exercise and provided some entertainment at the same time. We would punch each other in the body only, and we didn't hold back. Pike, however, had been a boxer in civilian life, so I think that I got the worst of these exchanges.

Memorable, also, was the mess-hall lineup. New Zealand lamb, prepared in one way or another, was a staple, and after a while it became very monotonous. To show our frustration and dissatisfaction, a chorus of "Baa! Baa! Baa!" echoed up and down the chow line.

In our exasperation with endless parade-square training, we got more and more unruly, and made a mockery of army rules and discipline. When the sergeant-major shouted, "On parade!" we'd bend at the waist and do our best to imitate Groucho Marx's unique walk.

One day the sergeant-major called us all out on parade. He was furious! He called us to attention, and then began bellowing. "Because of your foolish antics," he shouted, "I got shit on from a *great height!*" It was all we could do to keep from laughing. I remembered, almost nostalgically, the fearsome Sergeant MacDougal, from my old artillery unit, back in Canada. This sergeant did a creditable imitation of him, but I realized that I had finally changed: I was no longer afraid of sergeants. Nevertheless, we were still in the army, so we had to listen to his bluster and try to look contrite.

We had to retrain on Canadian weapons, even though— given the late stages of the war—we considered the whole procedure to be a charade. After a couple of months of Canadian weapons training, we were shipped to the First Canadian Parachute Battalion's headquarters in Bulford, on Salisbury Plains. The battalion was engaged in the invasion of

Germany. We were used as instructors, because we were experienced veterans.

We were in Bulford when the war ended. The joy and excitement was indescribable. Everyone shouted, laughed, and kissed and hugged each other; even the stiff upper lip of the English quivered a little with emotion after six years of struggle and deprivation!

I got a leave to Belfast, a few days later, but I couldn't go to Southern Ireland, because it had been a neutral country during the war. The green hills of the countryside were rejuvenating, and Belfast fascinated me as places steeped in history always do. My strongest memory from my visit, though, is of a less abstract gratification. I saw a vendor on the street selling ice-cream. It was wonderful, but don't get me wrong. It wasn't near as good as that at MacLaughlin's Ice-Cream Parlour in Truro! Maybe the real reason I remember the ice-cream is that I'd no sooner finished it than I saw two MPs approaching. My God, I thought, was I in hot water again? "You're First Can. Para., aren't you? All your unit is ordered back to camp!"

I returned to Bulford reluctantly; had it been earlier in the war I might well have decided, again, that a bit of freedom was more important to me than obeying orders. But I guess that I suspected something momentous might be happening, and when I got back to camp I shared everyone's elation at the news that we were *going home to CANADA!!*

Chapter 27
Home

The First Canadian Parachute Battalion boarded the huge ship *Isle De France* at Glasgow, Scotland. There were thousands of service people aboard—both men and women, from army and airforce. I could feel the excitement, joy, and anticipation throughout the ship.

Wouldn't it be a miracle, I thought, if I could meet someone from Truro? The very next day I ran into Lloyd MacPhee and we greeted like long-lost brothers, although we didn't know each other well. That I should meet him, of all people, immediately became significant for me: Lloyd was Greta's brother, so I took it as a good sign, and looked forward more than ever to seeing her again.

From the moment I'd heard we were going home, I'd begun to speculate about our possible future together. Would she still be interested in me? Was I reading things into our friendship that weren't there? These questions were more insistent by the time we were actually on our way home, so meeting Lloyd did seem something of a portent.

I didn't breathe a word of this to him, though, in case nothing happened between me and Greta. But I had to bite my tongue when he told me that he was going to do so much for his family, especially his only sister. He was going to take her to restaurants and the movies—really show her a good time.

I'd also known Lloyd's brother, Mosher, very well. We had trained together at Fort Benning, Georgia, where we had both earned our paratrooper's wings. Mosher had stayed in the

First Canadian Parachute Battalion when I transferred into the First Special Service Force, and he had been among the first soldiers to land in France on D-day. He was one of a select group of paratroopers called "The Pathfinders" who parachuted in after midnight in order to secure the drop zone for the main body of paratroopers that was to follow. Mosher survived this dangerous mission, but his luck ran out two months later. He was leading a patrol across an open field when he was struck on the shoulder by a rifle grenade and killed almost instantly. His family learned later that Mosher was to have been commissioned the following day.

Lloyd and I had plenty of things to talk about. He told me the misadventurous circumstances that led to his spending one year in Germany as a prisoner of war. He'd been captured the day after D-day. His captors marched him many miles, then, to his amazement, fell into an exhausted sleep when they sat down to rest. So of course he ran, as fast as his legs would carry him, back to where he thought his unit (the North Nova Scotia Highlanders), was positioned. He saw a lone jeep coming down the road, and he rushed out and hailed it down before he realized that its two occupants were wearing strange uniforms and helmets—and their guns were aimed at him! He was a prisoner of war in Germany until he was liberated by the Russians one year later. When he returned to England, he was reunited with his girlfriend, Frances Bogie. A few days later they had gotten married, and now they were temporarily parted because Lloyd had to return to Canada, where Frances would soon join him.

I remember little else about our Atlantic crossing, but one thing that sticks in my mind is the eating arrangements. (What else would you expect Peppard to remember, my buddies would say.) We had two meals a day, but because there were so many passengers, it was an assembly line. We ate in shifts. We were called out in groups, and after one group finished the first meal of the day, the next group was called out. The

process was repeated for the second meal of the day. The mess hall was full at all times. It must have been a nightmare for the cooks and dishwashers!

It was a beautiful summer day, June 22, 1945, when we caught our first glimpse of Canada. Shouting and cheering, we slapped each other on the back and embraced friend and stranger alike. As we steamed into Halifax harbour, many boats came out to greet us. Fireboats shot streams of water hundreds of feet into the air, and a band struck up from the shore as the *Isle de France* nosed into Pier 21. The cheering crowd on the dock, the music, the fireboats—it was an overwhelming welcome! Everyone rushed to the port side of the ship to try to catch a glimpse of a familiar face, and to be more a part of the moment. A crackling command over the ship's loudspeaker cut through the thousands of happy voices. "Now hear this! Now hear this! Will some of you *please* get over to the other side of the ship. We are in danger of capsizing!" Reluctantly, some of us moved to the starboard of the ship. The hint of panic in the voice and the message impressed us.

As we debarked I looked for familiar faces, but of course

my family didn't even know that I was coming home. The First Canadian Parachute Battalion was the first complete army unit to return to Canada from overseas, and we had been told we would be parading through Halifax. Coming down the gangplank I kept scanning the crowd, praying that I would see a familiar face. I didn't really expect to, but I hoped against hope, and when we walked into the cavernous terminal at Pier 21 I came face to face with my brother-in-law, Loran Morrison! Loran was a huge man, six feet four inches and the picture of health and power.

Loran was in the navy, and he had a Shore Patrol (SP) armband on his sleeve. He was the navy equivalent to an MP, and such a formidable man that I thanked my lucky stars I'd never met his likes on any of my escapades. His smiling face capped off my homecoming. Through him I found out all about my family. It was hard to pull away from him.

Our parade through Halifax more than made up for my disappointment that I hadn't been able to march into Rome alongside my buddies in the First Special Service Force. This was the hero's welcome I'd craved! Our countrymen lined the streets, cheering wildly, as we high stepped along—our jump-boots shining, our uniforms immaculate, maroon berets cocked at a jaunty angle. We must have been an impressive sight! I was so excited that I don't remember my boots even hitting the cobblestone streets.

A dignitary—Mayor Ahern, I think—presented our commanding officer, Colonel Eadie, with the keys to the city. I didn't know exactly what that meant, but I felt that it was a great honour nevertheless. We were dismissed in front of a string of barracks, where we were to spend the night.

I rushed for the nearest phone to call home. I could hear the ring on the other end, and my heart was beating faster. Someone lifted the receiver and said hello. It was Mum. I was so overcome with emotion that I could hardly speak. "Hi Mum, it's me!" I shouted. There was silence at the other end of the line, and then she yelled: "Herbie, where are you? Are you in Canada?" "Yes, Mum, I'm in Halifax. We just got back today!" "When will you be home!" "Tomorrow, on the first train out of Halifax!" "We'll all be at the station to meet you!"

The train trip home took less than two hours, but to me it seemed more like two weeks. The train stopped at every little station. Would it ever speed up a little? Didn't the engineer know my family was waiting? Close to Stewiacke I gazed out the window, and there on a hill was a huge billboard that showed two men, dressed in longjohns, each grasping the other's hand as if they were hand-wrestling. Above the figures, in bold letters, was the sign "Stanfield's Underwear." If I'd doubted it before, I doubted no longer—I was *Home!*

As the train pulled into the Truro station, I scanned the crowd on the platform, but I didn't have to look long, because a family of ten is a crowd in itself. They were all frantically waving, and in no time I was in the midst of them, being hugged by everyone! We all cried, laughed, shouted, whispered, and talked at once! I cast a few furtive glances around the platform, praying that Greta too had come down to greet me. But she was nowhere to be seen.

As we walked home to Alice Street, I held my little brother Billy's hand. Billy was nine years old, and I'm sure that he looked up to his big brother as some kind of hero; but he must have wondered, on that day, why the hand that held his was trembling, and why I was shaking like a leaf.

When I opened the gate at 17 Alice Street and strolled into our yard, I knew for sure that I was safe and sound. The ten maples that ringed the house I'd grown up in were in full foliage, green and fresh. The little lattice-work summerhouse with the vines creeping up it was exactly as I'd remembered it. The garden that Dad planted was laid out in perfectly straight rows, as only Dad could do it. The house, which was Mum's domain, was spotless. The shiny wood stove, with

Herb with his parents and his sister Patricia (a W.A.C. in Canadian Army).

its attached reservoir, reminded me of many a succulent family meal. I caught the aroma of roast chicken in the air, and my mouth started to water immediately! I knew every nook and cranny in this house, as though it were a part of myself.

With my parents and family around me, in our family home, I had a deep feeling of security and peace. I don't remember kneeling down, but I did close my eyes. In my mind's eye I reviewed my war experiences. I realized that I had been truly blessed to be able to return home, safe and sound. With my eyes still closed, I offered up a prayer of thankfulness and gratitude. I repeated over and over to myself: "Thank God I'm Home! Thank God I'm Home!"

Enjoying the peace: Herb, his younger brother Billy and his companion-in-arms George Traitt, in Montreal after V-E Day.

Chapter 28

All's Well That Ends Well

I was home for two days before I got up enough nerve to visit Greta. They had been wonderful days, spent visiting relatives and friends and basking in the love and togetherness of family. Mum's cooking was an added bonus, especially the biscuits and butter tarts I'd longed for so many times while I was away.

Nighttime in the privacy of my room was a little different. A beautiful face would appear in my mind's eye, and a desperate longing would flood over me. I wondered whether I could ever win the heart of such a gorgeous woman. I was determined to try, in spite of warnings from my sisters.

Maybe they were just warning me so that I wouldn't feel too much of a letdown. They said that they'd seen Greta going steady with a fellow from the airforce, and that they seemed very, very close. Needless to say, that dampened my spirits and nearly shattered my dreams; for, if she was in love with someone else, then I had no chance at all. Maybe that explained why I hadn't received a letter from her in months, and why she hadn't come to the station to meet me.

Would I swallow my pride and go down to the telephone office, where she worked, to see her? I was terrified that she would reject me. I didn't know if my pride could stand that. That old saying kept going through my head: "Faint heart ne'er won fair lady!" Well, if there were any fainter heart in the world, I wouldn't want to see it! Was she worth that risk? Damn right she was!

I strode into the telephone office the next day. In the

entryway, I knocked on a glass-panelled door. My heart was in my throat; my stomach was churning. This was worse than going into action. My life wasn't at stake, but my heart was. I stood there shaking like a leaf in a strong wind. And who should answer the door but Greta herself!

I really wasn't prepared for it. I had carried her picture with me all the time that I was overseas; I had pictured her in my mind's eye many, many times. I knew that she was a beautiful woman, but I couldn't believe how beautiful she really was. I felt like crushing her in my arms, but that would have been embarrassing to us both if I found that she loved someone else.

I sat down on some steps while we were talked. I didn't want Greta to see how nervous I was. I clasped my hands together to keep them from shaking. As I looked at her gorgeous face and figure, I thought to myself, "No way, Herb, are you ever going to win this wonderful creature!" We must have talked for about half an hour. I wondered what her boss, Mr. Bulmer, thought about that. Maybe he was so patriotic that he didn't begrudge Greta spending half an hour with a veteran.

Before I left, I saw something in those beautiful blue eyes that I just couldn't believe. It looked to me like a flicker of interest, a glow of tenderness. Did I dare to hope that I really had a chance? Greta agreed to let me walk her home that night.

As I walked proudly up Young Street alongside Greta, I was the happiest I'd been in my entire life! When we came to Mr. Wooley's (He kept a beautiful garden), I couldn't resist stealing a beautiful pink rose for Greta. Although she was a little apprehensive, I knew that she was pleased.

We talked a lot—about her brother, Mosher (She had been the only one at home when the telegram came from the War Office. It had been a terrible blow to her, because she thought a great deal of her older brother.) and about my plans to go to vocational school in Halifax. I thought that the electrical trade looked very promising, and although I only had my grade nine, I was willing to do my very best to avoid returning to the lumberyard. The lumberyard had been in my past, and I wanted it to stay there. We talked about our lives, steering clear of mentioning boyfriends and girlfriends. I was thankful for that.

It was on our third date that I got up the courage to kiss Greta. I was very nervous, thinking that she might turn aside, or push me away. But miracle of miracles, she put her arms around me and returned my kisses! I couldn't believe it! Was this beautiful woman actually falling in love with me? This was beyond my wildest dreams!

After that, I went through the most difficult time of my life. My problem was sexual frustration. Greta would not have sexual relations with me. It was against all her principles and her upbringing. I, on the other hand, wasn't that pure, but neither was I very worldly wise.

I remember one particular night when we had been sitting on the chesterfield in her living room. The rest of her family were all in bed. It had been a blissful evening, full of hugs and tender kisses. However, as usual, that was as far as it went. I left Greta's house highly frustrated—angry with Greta, angry with myself, angry with the whole world. There was a big telephone pole just down the lane from her house. I had a maddening urge to smash my fist into that post with all my strength, thinking it might ease my frustrations and quiet the urges buried deep within me. It was only with great effort that I restrained myself.

No one had told me that love would be such a mixture of sweetness and hellish torture! Yet, as I walked further, an unbelievable thing happened! A voice spoke to me—a prophetic sounding but positive voice. It seemed to come from outside, but also from inside me. The voice said emphatically: "You're going to marry that girl! You're going to marry

Greta and I, July 1945, were looking foreward to our lives together. We were married in June 1946.

that girl!" This came like a thunderbolt out of the blue. How stupid of me! Of course that's what Greta wanted—and that's what I *wanted!* All the while I was overseas, I had treasured my dream of having a beautiful, faithful wife, and a cosy little family. That's what I wanted, and that's what I had hoped to get. So what was I thinking of? What was holding me back?

Absolutely nothing! I proposed to my beautiful girl the very next day. When she accepted me my spirits soared, and our future looked boundless!

In no time at all, it seemed, I was standing by my beautiful bride-to-be in the First United Church Manse, on Queen Street, in Truro. Rev. Earl Gordon was the minister. I was much more nervous than Greta, but I managed to stumble through my vows.

As I stood there I recalled that only a little more than a year before I had been lying in the muck and mire of fox-holes, cringing in fear while artillery shells exploded close by. Now, I stood in this peaceful manse next to the most beautiful girl in the world and surrounded by family. Greta was smiling at me, as though she could read my thoughts, and my heart was almost bursting with pride and joy!

I thanked God that I had been so lucky. There had been so many times throughout the war when I might have been killed, or taken a turn at the crossroads of fate that would have led me away from meeting Greta and being here with her today. Too many to mention!

My heart was in my throat and I was choked with emotion as the ceremony continued. When Reverend Gordon asked, "Do you take Greta Eileen to be your lawful wedded wife?" I choked back a sob and shakily answered: "I do!" when in my heart I wanted to shout my true feelings to the whole world: "I do! ! do! I do! I do!"

Epilogue

Most veterans prefer to recall the humour of those dark days from 1939 to 1945. Number me amongst them. Sometimes, however, the stark reality of war is brought home to us— even years later. Such was the grim reminder I had just the other day. Without realizing it, I found myself standing in front of the town's cenotaph. We often walk past this monument to our heroic dead, without even glancing at it. This day was different. I felt that the hand of fate, or maybe a feeling of guilt, had guided me to this sacred place. I bowed my head for a minute or two. Then I looked at the names of the boys I had known. I ran my fingers along the deep grooves in the granite. Names of friends of mine. I could picture them in my mind's eye: young, smiling, healthy—alive.

I touched the name "Gerald Hamilton." Gerald was my next-door neighbour. He had joined the Royal Canadian Air Force while very young. He became an air-gunner in a bomber and was shot down early in the war. He was eighteen. The next name to catch my attention was "Billy Stevenson." Billy was in the Royal Canadian Navy serving on the destroyer *St. Croix*. His ship was sunk by a German U boat in the Gulf of St. Lawrence. Billy was not among the survivors. He was nineteen. The name "Mosher MacPhee" was a dear one to me. Mosher and I trained together as paratroopers. After the war I married his sister, Greta, so Mosher would have been my brother-in-law. Mosher was in the First Canadian Parachute Battalion. While leading a patrol across an open field, he was struck on the shoulder by a rifle grenade. He died almost instantly—age twenty-three!

I wiped tears from my eyes as I left the cenotaph. These young men never had the privilege of raising a family and watching their children grow up. They died while still boys themselves. As I walked away from the cenotaph, the words of a poem kept going through my mind. It was the verse of a poem adopted by the Royal Canadian Legion, and by many legions throughout the world. It goes like this:

> They shall grow not old, as we that are left grow old
> Age will not weary them nor the years condemn
> At the going down of the sun, and in the morning
> We will remember them.

(left to right) Tom Prince, Dave Hoskins and "Spud" Wright remember their comrades at a Force reunion, Thunder Bay, 1976.